HAUNTED
SCUNTHORPE

HAUNTED
SCUNTHORPE

Jason Day

The
History
Press

First published 2010

The History Press
The Mill, Brimscombe Port
Stroud, Gloucestershire, GL5 2QG
www.thehistorypress.co.uk

British Library Cataloguing in Publication Data.
A catalogue record for this book is available from the British Library.

ISBN 978 0 7524 5521 1
Typesetting and origination by The History Press
Printed in Great Britain

Contents

About the Author

Writer and Broadcaster Jason Day was born and raised in Scunthorpe, where he lived for nearly thirty years until moving to Essex. Jason was the longest serving feature writer for *Paranormal* magazine (March 2006-January 2008), the largest monthly paranormal publication of its kind in the UK at the time, writing over twenty articles during that period. He has also been a regular contributor to paranormal publications such as *FATE* magazine in the USA (the longest running paranormal magazine in the world) and *Ghost Voices* magazine in the UK. Jason's first paranormal book *It's Only A Movie…Isn't It?* (Phantom Encounters, May 2010) was released earlier this year. Jason also works with others in the written media, including some very prominent names in the paranormal community.

His interest in the paranormal was sparked by his love of film and passion for reading. Jason grew up on a staple diet of *Hammer Horror* movies and the written works of Peter Underwood, Dr Hans Holzer and Harry Price. With the advent of television shows such as *Arthur C. Clarke's Mysterious World* and *Strange But True* Jason was hooked. He decided to begin researching and investigating cases of the paranormal for himself and the fuse was lit.

Jason's experience working in the paranormal field has been varied, ranging from being a regular co-host on the *Friday Night Paranormal Show* on Pulse Talk Radio to being the featured article writer for the paranormal reference website ghostdatabase. co.uk. Jason is also the chief consultant for the Famously Haunted Awards organisation on MySpace. He has been a guest on several radio shows, appeared at many paranormal events and given lectures about his work within the paranormal field and the subject of the paranormal in general.

Jason currently hosts *The White Noise Paranormal Radio Show* on Blog Talk Radio and has interviewed such figures in the paranormal community as James Randi, Dr Ciaran O'Keeffe, Derek Acorah, Nick Pope, Stanton Friedman, Richard Wiseman, Ian Lawman, Jason Karl and Richard Felix. Now in it's third series and well on it's way to a hundred episodes, the show can be found live online every Friday night from 10 p.m. to midnight on the Blog Talk Radio website at http://blogtalkradio.com/famously-haunted, or alternatively at the Official White Noise Radio Show Website (http://www.whitenoiseparanormalradio.co.uk). Jason and the show recently won two awards at the International Paranormal Acknowledgment Awards 2009. Jason was named Best International Paranormal Radio Show Host and *The White Noise Paranormal Radio Show* was voted Best International Paranormal Radio Program.

One of three founding members of a small not-for-profit organisation based in Essex (SPIRIT, Society for Paranormal Investigation, Research, Information and Truth – established March 2006), Jason's commitment to researching, investigating and the search to explain the paranormal has expanded with the formation of the paranormal events company Phantom Encounters Limited in 2010. Members of the public can join Jason and the team on ghost hunts, UFO sky watches and monster hunts to gain greater 'hands on' knowledge of investigating the paranormal (http://www.phantomencounters.co.uk). You can find out more about Jason at his official website (http://www.jasonday.co.uk).

Jason Day (right) interviewing former Most Haunted Sensitive Ian Shillito (left) at the Phantom Encounters Lecture Series in Essex (July 2009). (Photograph by Dave Cable)

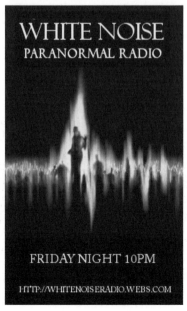

Jason hosts the White Noise Paranormal Radio Show every Friday night.

Foreword

Being an author, writer and paranormal expert myself, I have travelled far and wide in search of the unexplained. There are believers and there are sceptics but one thing seems constant, and that is that many people have pre-conceived ideas of where you are most likely to experience something paranormal.

Talk of ghosts and hauntings often conjures up visions of spooky castles and dark, dank tunnels from an age gone by. These locations are often found in places like Scotland or the South East of England. Think of North Lincolnshire, and in particular Scunthorpe, and ghosts are probably the furthest thing from your mind. Pictures of cooling towers billowing smoke into the atmosphere from the town's steelworks and the humdrum of life in a Northern town probably come to mind. Yet the town and its surrounding area have a vast history of paranormal activity.

Ghostly experiences have been reported and documented in and around the town since the 1700s, and continue to this day. There are stories of phantom animals, malicious poltergeists and spooky children to be found should one look hard enough. Scunthorpe and the North Lincolnshire area are also home to some of England's most interesting and more famous hauntings. Amongst these are an on-going haunting spanning three generations and nearly thirty years of paranormal activity.

There is also the case of the Epworth Poltergeist from the eighteenth century, the most documented poltergeist case in English history to date.

An overview of modern-day Scunthorpe.

Jason Day has painstakingly researched such cases since his youth. Jason was born and grew up in Scunthorpe and is regarded as one of the area's prominent experts in the paranormal field. Being a proud 'Scunthonian', he very much wanted to give the town something back and show it in a positive light. I'm sure you will agree with me that he has managed to achieve this with his excellent ghostly guide to Scunthorpe and the surrounding area.

So join Jason as he takes you on a tour of the area where you will encounter phantom airmen, ghostly nurses and spooky steelworkers. Take a ride on a ghost train or join the long deceased airmen who still patrol the skies in their phantom bombers. Enter such locations as haunted homes, churches, hospitals and factories. Read real case histories from actual paranormal investigation reports and much more in a book containing over fifty spooky stories from haunted Scunthorpe. You'll love it!

Jacky Newcomb, 2010
www.JackyNewcomb.com

Jacky is one of the UK's leading experts on the paranormal, as well as a multi-award winning *Sunday Times* best-selling author, columnist and television presenter.

A Brief History of Scunthorpe

Scunthorpe is a town within North Lincolnshire and has an estimated total resident population of around 72,500. The town itself lies on a rich bed of iron ore and limestone – crucial in the manufacturing of steel.

The earliest evidence of settlements in the area date back to the Bronze Age but it was not until the Roman occupation of Britain that ironstone was discovered in the area. The Romans originally mined the seams but with their departure the iron ore lay forgotten until the nineteenth century.

Records dating back to the Domesday Book (1086) reveal that the town took its name from the Hamlet of Escumetorp, which is Old Norse for 'Skuma's homestead', a site which is believed to be in the town centre close to where the present-day Market Hill in Scunthorpe is located. With the iron-ore deposits still to be rediscovered, the town became a small agricultural area. In fact, Scunthorpe at this time was not even the largest of the five townships which were to make up the modern borough. Ashby was, and the total population of the five villages (Crosby, Scunthorpe, Frodingham, Brumby and Ashby) at the 1851 Census was a mere 1,245.

That is until 1859, when Roland Winn stumbled across the ore on his father's land. The rediscovery of iron ore resulted in the development of an iron and steel industry and rapid population growth.

Iron ore was first mined in the Scunthorpe area in July 1860. Owing to the lack of a mainline railway, the ore was transferred to a wharf at Gunness (or Gun House), initially by cart then by a narrow-gauge railway, for distribution by barge or mainline rail from Keadby. Roland Winn knew that the best way of exploiting the iron-ore fields was for a rail link to be built from Keadby to Barnetby. He campaigned tirelessly for the link; construction work started in mid-1860 and was complete in 1864. He persuaded the Dawes brothers, to whose ironworks the ore was being supplied, to build an ironworks at the site of the iron-ore fields at Scunthorpe. Construction of Scunthorpe's first ironworks, the Trent Ironworks, began in 1862, with the first cast from the blast furnace being tapped on 26 March 1864. Other ironworks followed: building of the Frodingham Ironworks began in 1864; North Lincoln Ironworks in 1866; Redbourn Hill Iron & Coal Co. in 1872; Appleby Ironworks blew in their first blast furnace in 1876; the last one constructed was John Lysaght's Iron and Steelworks in 1911, with production starting in 1912. Crude steel had been produced at Frodingham Ironworks in 1887 but this proved not to be viable. Maxmilian Mannaburg came to

Frodingham Ironworks in 1889 to help build and run the steel-making plant, and on the night of 21 March 1890 the first steel was tapped.

Rowland Winn assumed the title Lord St Oswald in 1885 and is remembered in the town by three street names: Rowland Road, Winn Street and Oswald Road.

In 1936 the five villages of Ashby, Brumby, Frodingham, Scunthorpe and Crosby combined together and became incorporated as the borough of Scunthorpe. The new borough also received a grant of a coat of arms from the College of Arms. These arms were transferred to the new borough council formed in 1974 and are now used by the town's charter trustees.

The green shield and golden wheat sheaf in the coat of arms recall that the area was, until recently, predominantly agricultural in nature. Across the centre of the shield is a length of chain. This represents the five villages linking together as one. At the top of the shield are two fossils of the species *gryphoea incurva*. These remains of oysters, known as the 'devil's toenails', were found in the rock strata from which ironstone was quarried. The crest, on top of the helm, shows a blast furnace. This is also referred to in the Latin motto: *Refulget labores nostros coelo* or 'The heavens reflect our labours', popularly attributed to the glow observed in the night sky from the steel-making activities.

During this time of local government reorganisation the Municipal Borough of Scunthorpe was the largest town in North Lindsey, known throughout the world for its latest contribution to the British steel industry, the giant Anchor works. The population, which had risen to 60,000 people by the 1970s, were looking to a prosperous future in steel.

By the latter half of the 1980s most of the economically viable seams of iron ore were mined and quarried and most raw materials are now imported. Currently the 'heyday' of Scunthorpe's steel industry is a bygone era, and although the steelworks are still in production, they appear to be in decline.

So what of Scunthorpe's modern history?

The Scunthorpe coat of arms,
c. 1936.

In the computer age the town of Scunthorpe made a piece of history itself, if not entirely through choice or for the good of modern technology. In 1996 there was controversy when internet provider America on Line's obscenity filter (among others) refused to accept the name of the town due to its inclusion of a stream which the filter rejected as obscene. Some online forums such as Ultimate Guitar forums (which has since been resolved) display the name as S★★★horpe, while Fark.com would display it as Scoonthorpe. This situation is known in the computing world as the 'Scunthorpe problem' and is still an issue to some Scunthorpe-based internet users.

Another noteworthy episode in the town's history occurred on 27 February 2008 when Scunthorpe was close to the epicentre of one of the largest earthquakes experienced in the British Isles. Significant shocks were felt in Scunthorpe and the surrounding North Lincolnshire area. The main 10-second quake, which struck at 0056 GMT at a depth of 15.4km (just over nine and a half miles), was the biggest recorded example since one with a magnitude of 5.4 struck north Wales in 1984. Some buildings were damaged in the town but fortunately there were no human casualties.

With a history of over 4,000 years, the town has experienced many ups and down and many people have been born, lived and died in Scunthorpe. Some of them even continue to reside in the town and surrounding villages long after their deaths...

In the following pages you will encounter some of these 'ghostly' residents of Scunthorpe, the buildings they inhabit and the stories behind the hauntings. This book will take you through the history of the town and its surrounding area that many books choose to omit, the haunted history of Scunthorpe.

1

The Ghosts of Scunthorpe

Spirits of the Inn – Ashby Star

Licensed premises are an often cited location for paranormal activity and usually there is an abundance of them in any given area. Curiously, whilst researching this book, when looking into pubs and inns in Scunthorpe I was met with a dearth of hauntings. It would seem that either the licensees of the premises are reluctant to talk about any ghostly goings-on in their establishments, or that the spirits of Scunthorpe are 'tee-total'.

One public house in Scunthorpe that has reported paranormal activity is the Ashby Star on Rochdale Road. The Star is a relatively young pub in terms of how long it has been established as an inn, being built in 1958. That said, there appears to have been no shortage of paranormal incidents in the building, with both staff and customers reporting strange activity over the last fifty years.

Eerie shadows, the movement of objects by unseen hands and unexplained noises are amongst the list of phenomena that has allegedly occurred within the building. In an attempt to try to find out who or what was causing the disturbances a team of paranormal investigators were called in, and on the 27 June 2009 P.P. Paranormal Investigators carried out an overnight investigation at the pub.

During the night the team set up various experiments including sealing off a room which contained two motion detectors (the theory being if anything

The sign outside the Ashby Star.

moved in the room the detectors would be activated and they would know something or someone was in there). The motion detectors were triggered twice during the investigation, even though the room remained sealed from any outside interference.

The team also conducted a séance, and whilst doing so they heard banging that seemed to have no explainable source. A medium who was present on the night also claimed to pick up on some spirits in the building during the investigation: the medium believed that the spirits may even have been directly connected to the people that ran the pub at the time (as opposed to the building itself).

Whether the ghosts that haunt the Ashby Star are connected to the staff or the building, with regular reports of activity spanning half a century, it would appear that they will continue to occupy the building for some time to come.

The Scunthorpe Poltergeist – Avenue Vivian

Poltergeist activity is probably one of the most disturbing forms of paranormal phenomena. A poltergeist is believed to be a noisy, mischievous spirit which manifests itself by causing objects to move, and/or physical damage. The phenomena is often linked to a teenage child and believed to draw its strength from the emotion and angst of the child going through the final steps into adulthood. These cases are usually short lived, with the paranormal activity often fading away within months of phenomena commencing.

Frustratingly, the issue surrounding one reported case of this phenomena occurring in Scunthorpe is that the details and facts of the case are few and far between; this is largely due to the incident having occurred at a time when the subject of hauntings was not so readily accepted by a more cynical society.

Avenue Vivian, home to the 'Scunthorpe Poltergeist' during the 1970s.

What is known is that the case occurred in 1973 in a family home in Avenue Vivian. The haunting bore all the hallmarks of a typical poltergeist infestation. The activity began with loud bangs and knocking on the walls of the house without any apparent cause. The next stage of the haunting involved the movement of objects, including heavy furniture, around the home. In one instance it was reported that a sofa in the home, which was still covered in plastic sheeting, was seen to show an indentation which had no visible cause. It was as if an invisible presence had sat down on it.

One apparition was apparently witnessed in the home: the manifestation of a curly-haired boy wearing brown clothing was reportedly seen during the haunting.

Little more is known of the case; if any other families that later occupied the property had any similar experiences it is likewise unknown.

Witches, Graveyards and Ghosts – Bottesford

Bottesford is a civil parish and small town to the south of Scunthorpe, which, until the twentieth century, was a small farming village. Bottesford is mentioned in the Domesday Book under the name 'Budlesford', and was also the location of Bottesford Preceptory (which, it is said, the Knight's Templar of St John used as a base). The word 'preceptory' is used for the community of the Knights Templar which lived on one of the order's estates in the charge of its preceptor. From that its meaning was extended to include the estate and its buildings. The present Bottesford Manor is believed to have been the gatehouse to the preceptory.

Templars Bath, a spring in the field behind Bottesford Manor is now hardly discernible, being simply a gathering of stones. The bath has been attributed to the Romans but others believe it was a dipping bath or well used by the Templar workers.

Other local features include Bottesford Beck and St Peter ad Vincula. Having such a vast history, it would come as no surprise to find that the town of Bottesford has had its fair share of hauntings – and that is indeed the case.

The land on which number 214 Bottesford Lane now sits is the site of a former cottage. The front wall of the garden is actually built upon the remains of the building. Local legend says that the old cottage was occupied by a woman believed to be a witch, and the children of Bottesford at the time were warned to stay away from her home.

Another local legend involves paranormal activity that is said to occur in the graveyard of the church of St Peter ad Vincula. Within the churchyard is a tombstone that was once surrounded by iron railings. The railings that encircled the grave have long since gone, as has the inscription on the gravestone that identified the poor soul that was laid to rest beneath it. Legend has it that if you put your ear against the headstone you can hear the jangling of chains. Is this the sound of 'residual energy' from a past time when the railings surrounded the grave? Or is the noise coming from beneath the ground and grave within it?

Perhaps the most intriguing paranormal story involving the area is that of the haunting of Bottesford Beck. The Beck is a stream that runs through the town, and it was along the Beck that a servant girl was murdered whilst returning to a farm in the area several hundred years ago. For some time after the murder, horses crossing the Beck were reported to rear up in fright and turn around in the road, refusing to cross the bridge. Often handlers would have to physically lead their horses across the Beck.

The haunted graveyard at St Peter ad Vincula Church in Bottesford.

The church of St Peter ad Vincula, Bottesford.

The former site of an alleged witch's house in Bottesford.

Bottesford Beck's haunted bridge.

Other animals would behave strangely in this area too. Cattle that grazed near the Beck kept away from the crossing place (perhaps because animals are more sensitive to the presence of spirits?).

More recently, there have been reports of the apparition of a young woman in the area of the footbridge that crosses the Beck just behind St Peter's Church. Is the ghost of the servant girl still haunting the place of her death?

Wandering Spirits – Brumby Hospital/Café Ivy

The Café Ivy is a catering project, which is run through Mencap Education and Employment Business Unit in Scunthorpe. The project was started in July 2001 with their partner, North Lincolnshire Council. The café serves as a training facility for people with learning difficulties to learn catering, housekeeping, table service and all aspects of the catering trade, as well as holding Adult Education Classes in the building.

Formerly Brumby Hospital, Café Ivy is still said to be haunted.

The café is situated on the site of the old Brumby Hospital on East Common Lane and was founded in 1929. The hospital was originally called the Brumby Infectious Diseases Hospital and cared for tuberculosis sufferers, keeping them in isolation, between 1929 and 1955. Between 1955 and 1960 the building became the Brumby Infectious Diseases Hospital and Sanatorium, and (after 1948) became more of a long-stay facility. Later in life the hospital simply became Brumby Hospital and was a general medical facility before becoming the Café Ivy.

The first reported incident of paranormal activity came to light in March 1972. Whilst visiting the hospital in that year a mother and her child sensed the presence of a ghost in the car park. The pair were unable to identify whether the spirit was that of a man or a woman, but they were positive that the form they had witnessed was not that of anything of this world.

Following the transformation of the hospital into the café there was a second sighting of an apparition. The manager of the Café Ivy reported seeing a shadowy figure in the corridor one evening in 2004.

Were these sightings two different phantoms, or could this simply be one lonely wandering spirit who perhaps met their end in the old hospital?

Children Will Play – Cambridge House

Cambridge House is a social services centre on Cambridge Avenue in Bottesford. The building was formerly a children's home throughout the 1980s and 1990s with many children being placed in the care of the home throughout this period.

Cambridge House, Bottesford.

Haunted locations are said to be places where scenes of high emotion have occurred, the premise being that spirits feed on people's emotions in order to gain the energy to manifest as apparitions. Given this theory, the high levels of emotion involved in the social services centre, where people's problems are resolved and life-altering decisions are reached, could have attributed to the fact that it is now said to be haunted.

Having talked to members of staff who worked at the location, I have found that some claim to have encountered some very strange phenomena there indeed, particularly the physical movement of objects. Battery-operated toys which are kept at the centre have been witnessed to spring into life of their own accord: talking dolls have been activated with no apparent cause, and a toy bus once whizzed across the floor under its own steam. One member of staff placed a soft toy on a shelf with its back to the wall, but when they returned to the room to switch off the light and close the door they discovered that the soft toy was facing the wall. No one else was in the building at the time.

Another case in point is a member of staff who was cleaning up some paperwork in an office in 2009. As they did so, they noticed one of the office chairs had a coat resting over the back of it. The chair was facing the door, 'chair arms first'. The staff member left the room and closed the door. When they returned they found that the chair had swung around, with the back of the chair (with the coat still draped over it) now facing the door. When the member of staff checked with their colleague (the only other person in the building at the time), they confirmed that they had not been in the office in question at all that day.

Probably the most eerie encounter at Cambridge House is that of a member of staff who saw a shadowy figure on the stairs in January 2010. Again there were only two people in the building at the time, and the other person was accounted for. The witness saw the figure for only a split second before it disappeared.

The staff members I interviewed believe that the building is haunted by the ghost of a small child, possibly a young girl. Other members of staff who have 'heard and seen things' at Cambridge House say they tend to agree. The staff do not feel that the girl is a malicious or mischievous spirit; they believe she is just looking for a playmate to join in with her games.

The White Cylinder – Cemetery Road

Little is known about this alleged sighting, so suffice to say the details are vague to say the least. Sometime between the mid- to late 1900s a cyclist had a very unusual encounter on the very aptly named Cemetery Road in Scunthorpe.

Cemetery Road is located in the 'Old Brumby' area of Scunthorpe and derives its name from the large graveyard that is situated on one side of the street. It is reported that the man was cycling along this road one evening when what he described as a 'tall, white, cylindrical shape' crossed in front of him before vanishing. The terrified man then peddled off as fast as he could.

Perhaps the ghostly figure was returning to the cemetery from which he may have manifested?

The Haunted Home – Grange Lane South

Grange Lane South is a street in the Ashby area of Scunthorpe. The road is much like any other, flanked on either side by rows of three- and four-bedroomed terraced or semi-detached properties. The housing was originally built as council housing, but it has largely been bought out by tenants over the last twenty years or so. One house in particular may stand out from the others, though, and for very unusual reasons.

In October 2009 the Society of Paranormal Investigation, Research, Information and Truth (SPIRIT) received a phone call from the occupants of one of homes on the street reporting alleged paranormal activity in the property. The family claimed to have regular occurrences of objects moving of their own accord, unexplained noises and the occasional sighting of a shadowy figure. The family also reported that their daughter claimed to interact with a little girl in the house: was the little girl an imaginary friend of the child, or a spirit girl who had not moved on? After several phone calls and an interview at the property with the residents of the home, SPIRIT decided to investigate the property.

Grange Lane South, Scunthorpe.

Team members Jason and Kelly visited the home on the morning of the investigation to have a walk through of the property and a final consultation with the owners. It wasn't too long before something unusual occurred. As they left, one of the owners came running out of the house to catch up with Jason and Kelly. She asked them to come and look at something that had just appeared in the house. They went back into the house, where they discovered the other occupant of the house standing at the bottom of the stairs looking quite perplexed. The man pointed out a wet patch which had just appeared on the stairs; nothing that could have caused the patch could be discovered. Furthermore, sudden appearances of pools of water are a sign of poltergeist activity in some cases. The team took photos and a sample of the fluid before they left.

Later that afternoon Jason and Kelly returned with a medium. The medium had no previous knowledge of the history of the home, the occupants or where the home itself was located. Kelly stayed in the living room with the owners whilst Jason and the medium walked around the house. The medium relayed that he sensed the spirits of a small girl and a man in the property. He also pointed out that he felt there had been paranormal activity in the living room. As he walked past the closed living room door he said that there had been electrical appliances switching themselves on and off and 'cold spots' in the room. Jason and the medium then went upstairs – where, on the landing area, the medium said he felt the family had heard footsteps. He added that one (if not both) of the spirits that haunted the home had tried to make their presence known by manifesting on the landing. The residents may even have seen them as shadowy figures.

The medium detected that the spirit of the small girl most frequently appeared in the small bedroom; he added that she would have moved objects around in the room to try and make her presence felt, and that she also liked to play in this room. The bedroom adjacent to the small room was where the medium picked up on the most chilling information. He looked at the bed in the room and said that he felt whoever slept in this bed may have been moved by the spirit of the man whilst they were sleeping. He went as far as to say that they may have even been thrown from the bed by him on at least one occasion. Upon ending their walk around, Jason and the medium went downstairs and into the living room, where the medium met the owners of the house for the first time. Upon relaying his information to them he appeared to be startlingly correct. The owners confirmed all of the information the medium had relayed to Jason – including the fact that one of their children had indeed been inexplicably thrown from their bed one evening.

The haunted mirror where the face of a highwayman was seen.

The members of the SPIRIT team, including the medium, left the property again and headed back to brief the other team members and collect their equipment in readiness to return to investigate the property that evening.

The team, consisting of five investigators and a medium, returned to the house around 9 p.m. that evening. The only other people in the house were the couple who owned it. Various video cameras, temperature and humidity monitors and other monitoring equipment were set up around the building. A small table was put in the corner of bedroom where the child was allegedly thrown from their bed. On this table a cross and chain, an open Bible and other objects were placed. Talcum powder was then sprinkled all over the table so that if any of the objects moved, however slightly, it would be apparent. A video camera was pointed at the table and left to record any activity; the room was then sealed off. In the small bedroom 'paper dolls' were left on the floor at the foot of the bed in a specific arrangement in an attempt to see if the 'ghost' of the little girl would move them. Again another video camera was set up, this time at the far end of the landing opposite the small bedroom, to monitor the room for any activity (or catch any fraudulent behaviour). The door to this room was left open.

The team split into groups throughout the evening, changing locations and members intermittently. As the evening passed there were various interesting occurrences.

The 'paper doll'. This photograph was taken immediately after the doll was placed on the floor.

An experiment involving a mirror conducted in the living room had a rather alarming conclusion for one member of the team. The mirror was acquired from an allegedly haunted pub by the owner of the house and was hanging on the living room wall. SPIRIT team member Kyle decided to conduct a scrying experiment with the mirror. (Scrying is a form of divination that involves focusing your eyes as to try and 'see beyond' the mirror itself.) Whilst looking into the mirror Kyle began to see his features transform into that of a man with a 'tri-peaked' hat. Shaken by his experience, the investigator later concluded that the image he had seen could only be described as that of a highwayman.

More phenomena were to occur later. The 'paper dolls' in the small bedroom were found to have been moved from their original location and taken apart; even though a video camera had been monitoring the room the whole evening, it had not captured any of the investigators or the homeowners tampering with them. There was also no obvious explanation for the movement of the objects or their dissection (such as draughts or vibration).

When the sealed-off bedroom was inspected, SPIRIT discovered that objects in that room had also been displaced. The table that had been set up with trigger objects showed movement of some of the objects, most notably the Bible. The interesting thing about this occurrence was that the imprints left in the talcum powder would

This picture of the 'paper doll' was taken later in the evening and shows the doll has been taken apart. The room had been continuously monitored throughout the evening and nobody present in the house had touched the doll.

The table in the bedroom where objects had been mysteriously moved.

suggest that the Bible had been 'lifted' and replaced two or three times. As I mentioned earlier, the room had been sealed off and a video camera was 'locked on' to the table. After reviewing the footage, we discovered that no one had entered the room during the time the objects had been moved. There was no apparent earthly cause for the phenomena.

Throughout the night, various members of the team reported hearing unexplained knocks, feeling cold spots and other phenomena; the medium also relayed that he believed that the spirit of the small girl was actually present in the house that night. Another incident that took place during the investigation may lend weight to his claim.

As Jason checked the video camera in bathroom at the end of the hallway (the one that faced the small bedroom), he bent over to look at the buttons on the side of the camera. Unbeknownst to Jason, at that very moment the medium told one of the owners of the house that he had just seen a small girl exit the master bedroom (i.e. the room that they were in). Kelly was also in the master bedroom and decided to look out of the doorway to see if she could see anything. As she walked into the corridor, Jason heard what he believed to be a female voice say 'ha ha'. Jason assumed it was Kelly playing a prank, as she was the only female nearby and the voice sounded like that of a little girl. However, Kelly was adamant that it wasn't her. Jason looked around the bathroom: the house was a semi-detached building, and there was no adjoining building to the wall behind him, only a small, closed window. The wall to his right had no window and faced the street; the house had a large front garden so the possibility of a voice coming from the street via that side of the room was also minimal. Jason had heard the voice to his left side, which had the wall of the master bedroom adjoining it. This is the room the medium, one of the owners and Kelly were in when the phenomena occurred. There were no small children in the house at the time. What made this occurrence even more intriguing was the fact that the voice was caught on the video camera footage too.

The SPIRIT team concluded their investigation on the night and headed back to analyse their findings. The team reached the conclusion that there were definitely some interesting findings at the location, both explainable and unexplainable. A local medium visited the property at a later date, and at present paranormal activity at the home has significantly decreased.

The Ghost Of Humphrey — Normanby Hall

Normanby Hall is a classic English mansion located five miles north of Scunthorpe. Set in 350 acres of country park containing a fishing lake, duck ponds, deer sanctuary and broad leaf woodland, the estate is an idyllic location for stories of hauntings.

The history of Normanby Park dates back to the seventeenth century when the original Hall building was situated there. The present building began construction in 1825 and was completed in 1830 under the instruction of Sir Robert Sheffield. The family moved out of the Hall in 1963 and the property is now under the care of North Lincolnshire County Council. According to local legend, at least one lost soul wanders amongst the Victorian walled garden, farming museum and miniature railway contained within the grounds.

The Normanby Park Estate.

The story recounted amongst the locals is that sometime during the 1700 or 1800s a man known as Humphrey was caught stealing from what is now known as the Normanby Park Estate. Despite his pleas that he was only trying to feed his starving family, he was sentenced to swift 'justice' by the estate's owners. Humphrey was beaten to death on the grounds of the estate by the gamekeepers as a warning to others who might consider stealing from the grounds in the future.

The Ironstone Cottage – North Lincolnshire Museum

North Lincolnshire Museum is located on Oswald Road in the centre of Scunthorpe. Due to its location, the museum is known to locals in the town as Scunthorpe museum. Having been opened on 31 August 1909, the museum is just over 100 years old and was founded around collections that were principally geological and archaeological. The service now cares for and interprets the full range of the region's heritage, including its natural, archaeological, social, historical, technological and architectural heritage.

The museum is also home to a reconstructed nineteenth-century Victorian ironworker's cottage. It is an exhibit that is the cause of much conjecture. There have been several reports involving the cottage with regards to the possibility of paranormal phenomena. Visitors to the museum have reported phantom noises and feelings of unease, as if they were not alone whilst walking through the cottage. Although the exact history or details of the alleged haunting are not known, several people have attested to the fact that they believe the ironstone cottage is haunted.

Upon making contact with staff at the museum, I found that they themselves have experienced nothing they consider to be paranormal, both in the museum as a whole and with reference to the cottage itself.

There could be several reasons for this discrepancy. Perhaps the visitors to the museum were mistaken or deluded. Perhaps the staff are trying to 'play the paranormal activity down', or maybe the spirits have yet to make their presence known to them. Only further investigation and time itself will tell if the ironstone cottage is indeed truly haunted.

The Disappearing Workman – Quibell Park

Quibell Park is a sports stadium located just off Brumby Wood Lane. Originally a cinder running track opened in 1965, Quibell Park now boasts, amongst other amenities, a grandstand, changing rooms, an eight-lane running track, three football pitches and even a velodrome. To add to its ever-growing list of accomplishments, it would seem that the facility may have omitted to mention another addition to its inventory: the presence of its very own ghost.

In 1989, a college student was riding his moped along the Kingsway Road and turned left onto Brumby Wood Lane. As he turned onto the road, his moped coughed and spluttered and came to a grinding halt at the top of the hill, just outside the entrance to Woodlands Crematorium. Much annoyed, the student dismounted the moped, took off his helmet, hung it off the handlebars and proceeded to push the bike down the hill.

As he began to push the moped down Brumby Wood Lane, he looked up and noticed a man walking just in front of him. The student assumed that as he had been so caught up in his moped breaking down that he hadn't seen the man as he turned the corner. The man was stockily built, had 'scraggly' shoulder length grey hair, and wore blue 'council worker' trousers and a high-visibility, reflective safety jacket. The student only saw him from behind and could not see his face at this time, but judging from what he could see of the man, he assumed him to be between forty and fifty years of age.

The student felt uneasy about the man walking in front of him. There was just something about him. There were no other people walking on either side of the road and the traffic was scarce. Although it was daylight hours, his feeling of unease grew.

The student took care to push his moped slowly down the hill, so as not to catch the man up. He also kept his head down most of the time, only glancing up occasionally. (That way, the student thought, if the man did look around, there was a minimum chance of making eye contact with him.) They reached the bottom of the hill and continued along the level part of Brumby Wood Lane. The student glanced up, and as he approached the part of the road where the entrance to Quibell Park is, he realised that the man was still walking in front of him. The student looked back down at the handlebars of his moped, thinking 'perhaps the man will turn into the entrance and go in there'. The student looked up once again, just a split second later, and the man

Quibell Park Stadium, Scunthorpe.

Brumby Wood Lane, haunt of the 'Disappearing Workman'.

had disappeared. He stopped in his tracks. He looked around. He looked to his left; the fence around the entrance to Quibell Park was a metal structure that you could see through. Beyond that was a vast open field with a path leading up to the grandstand and other structures. The man was nowhere to be seen on this side. There was no way he could have got out of sight in a split second had he headed that way. The student looked to his right; on this side he had the road, a path beyond that and a wooded area beyond the path. Again there was no way the man could have crossed the road and entered the wooded area and been lost to eyesight amongst the trees in a split second. The student looked in front of himself. The man could not have got to the end of Brumby Wood Lane and gone around the corner in a split second either. That left one more possibility. Although he was sure he had not passed the man at any point, and indeed that the man had not come to a halt and let him pass him either, the student turned around to look behind him. There was no sign of the man up the hill beyond him. The part of the path that the student now stood on was midway along the road, so, as with the path in front of him, there was no way the man could have got to the top of the hill behind him and gone around the corner either. The man had simply vanished.

The student continued his journey home, confused, a little bewildered and definitely a lot quicker than he had have done if he had not had this experience.

So who or what was the vanishing figure? Could he have been a workman who had met his end in the woods, on the road or during the construction of a building in Quibell Park? Perhaps he is a wandering soul who comes and goes from the nearby Woodlands Crematorium (which is situated at the top of the hill on Brumby Wood Lane)?

Whoever or whatever he was, this is certainly an odd case and, to date, it remains unexplained in my personal files.

The Guardian Shuck – Scotter Road

Scotter Road is located between Doncaster Road and Ferry Road, connecting the Crosby area of the town to the rest of Scunthorpe. The road is also the location for one of the more bizarre paranormal events of the twentieth century to occur in the town.

During the 1900s a very unusual encounter with a black shuck was reported along Scotter Road. A shuck is the name given to ghostly dogs; they are said to be malevolent, and to roam the country, and are discussed in more detail in a later section of the book. The unusual thing about the following ghostly dog encounter, however, is that this shuck was anything but hostile.

A woman was walking along the road when she noticed a gang of labourers in the distance. As she got closer to the men she felt very uneasy, as if they may be somehow about to cause her harm. Nervously she continued to travel up the road – but as she got closer to the labourers, a black dog appeared from nowhere, and began walking alongside her. The dog stuck close to the woman's leg, so as to be in-between her and the men as she passed them. The guardian shuck continued to accompany her until she

A Blafphemer turn'd into a black Dog pa. 4.

This engraving, from Burton's 1685 collection Wonderful Prodigies, shows an unusual twist on the Black Dog myth: a blasphemer who cursed God for killing his cattle was transformed into a jet-black hound which fell upon the corpses of the beasts and devoured them. (Courtesy of Liam Quin, www.fromoldbooks.org)

reached her home, when it then mysteriously vanished. Following her experience, the woman was convinced the dog had prevented her from being attacked by the labourers.

The Ghost Train – Scotter Road Viaduct

In 1865 a viaduct was constructed in Scunthorpe. This was around the same time that ironstone was discovered in the town, and therefore would accommodate the railway which would be needed to carry materials to and from the plant. The bridge was completed during the reign of Queen Victoria and ran across what is now Scotter Road.

Over the years there have been various reports of paranormal phenomena around the viaduct. Witnesses have testified to hearing a train passing over it late at night whilst walking along Scotter Road. When they look to see the train, the viaduct is completely empty.

Scotter Road Viaduct, 1910.

There have been no recorded incidents of accidents associated with the viaduct, which leaves one to wonder why this haunting occurs. Is this simply a residual haunting that people are witnessing, or is the train still making its regular journey in 'real time'?

The Phantom Nurse – Scunthorpe General Hospital

It is often said that spirits of the departed tend to haunt places of extreme emotion, be that happiness or sadness. One place where both emotions can be found in abundance is hospitals.

Scunthorpe General Hospital is situated in Cliff Gardens, and before undergoing vast expansion and modernisation was known as Frodingham Hospital. In 1975 Barbara Goodall was working part-time in the hospital as a SRN and RFN. One afternoon she was doing her rounds of the children's wards when she noticed the unfamiliar and rather peculiar smell of violets. Barbara assumed that, unbeknownst to her, a mother or other female relative had snuck into the ward to visit a child and slipped back out again. The smell, she thought, must have been their perfume. It was only after she had encountered this phenomena two or three more times that she became concerned enough to relate her experiences to other members of staff on the ward. What they told her was to alarm her even more.

The smell of 'old-fashioned' violet perfume is said to herald the sudden appearance of the ghost of a nurse who dates back to the days of the old Frodingham Hospital. The nurse manifests, wearing what is described as 'long clothes partially covered with a long white apron', and then simply vanishes before witness's eyes.

Little is know about the history of the phantom nurse, but it is assumed that in life she tended to the sick children on the ward. This is believed to be the case, as sightings usually coincide with a baby on the ward (often under six months of age) becoming desperately ill. After the nurse's visitation the child is said to recover. Although Barbara

Goodall's account is from 1975, the phantom nurse has been reportedly sighted in recent years.

The Spectral Steelworker – Scunthorpe Steelworks

Construction of Scunthorpe's first ironworks, the Trent Ironworks, began in 1862, with the first cast from the blast furnace being tapped on 26 March 1864. Other ironworks followed. Crude steel had been produced at Frodingham Ironworks in 1887, but this proved not to be viable. Maxmilian Mannaburg came to Frodingham Ironworks in 1889 to help build and run the steel-making plant, and on the night of 21 March 1890 the first steel was tapped – and the town was changed forever.

The steel industry is still the major employer in the area and the largest operator within it is the Indian-owned firm Corus. However, the industry has shrunk in recent years, following the closure of the Normanby Park works (also known as Lysaght's) and the huge Redbourn complex in the early 1980s; the number employed in the industry has fallen from 27,000 at its height to around 4,500 (not including outside contractors, such as Hanson plc) today. Despite this, it is still the major integrated steel works in Britain.

Parts of the expansive plant include the continuous casting plant and the blast furnace and rod mill. There have been many stories circulating within the town and the steelworks itself describing paranormal activity at the plant. Some stories may be 'urban legend', some may have been lost with the passage of time and some of the actual hauntings may have even ceased to exist (with the spirits moving on to the next realm?). Interestingly, after a recent interview I conducted with an employee of the steelworks, it appears there may still be at least one active haunting at the plant.

Scunthorpe Steelworks.

'Jim', a man in his late thirties and a welder on the steelworks for most of his working life, gave me the following information. Although he has not witnessed the phenomena himself, Jim has been told on many occasions of a phantom figure seen wandering within the confines of the Boss Plant at the steelworks. Colleagues have reported seeing a shadowy figure treading the walkway of the sixth floor numerous times, a phenomena that reportedly continues to this day.

The apparition could be attached to another part of the steelworks, the Queen Victoria blast furnace. On 4 November 1975, a tragic explosion occurred at the furnace while a large amount of molten metal was being poured into a torpedo ladle. Four workers were killed and some fifteen more were injured, some very seriously. Ultimately eleven men would lose their lives as a consequence of the disaster. Over the years many stories persisted of paranormal phenomena in this area of the plant, eventually dying down and fading away. It is, however, possible that the apparition said to be seen at the Boss Plant could indeed be one of the poor souls that lost their lives at the furnace thirty-five years ago. He may have moved on to this area of the site, still looking for his fallen workmates.

A Family Haunting – Shipton Road

Shipton Road is a street in the Ashby area of Scunthorpe. Consisting of a mixture of semi-detached and terraced properties it is very much like many other housing estates in the town. However, one property located on Shipton Road has a certain quality that sets it apart from all the others, for this house may in fact be the most haunted home in Scunthorpe, Lincolnshire – and perhaps even further afield. The haunted history of the house can be traced back over twenty-seven years and continues to this day. Whilst in comparison to some cases this may seem a short period of time, there has been a huge amount of documented paranormal activity that has occurred.

The first known recorded paranormal activity happened sometime between November 1983 and May 1984 when one of the occupants, Mrs Winifred Day, was abruptly awoken in the early hours of the morning. Mrs Day was woken by what she described as a feeling of having 'hands around her throat' and a choking sensation. Thinking she was being attacked, she called out to alert other members of the household. However, when they rushed to her bedroom and turned on the light they discovered there was nobody there: whoever, or whatever, had attacked Winifred had gone.

Following this incident, more unexplained phenomena began to occur in the Day household. One such common event involved the family's pet dogs, a black Labrador called Bess and a Jack Russell called Sadie, who on several occasions could be heard barking frantically upstairs. Upon investigation, members of the family would find both animals sitting in the corner of the small bedroom, facing a blank wall, barking and snarling. Although this was not the bedroom in which the incident involving Winifred occurred, once again no cause for the phenomena could be found. The only conclusion the family could reach at the time was that perhaps the animals, which are said to be more sensitive to such things, sensed something paranormal in the house.

Shipton Road, Scunthorpe.

Winifred Day sadly passed away in January 1987, leaving only her husband Barry and their youngest two children living at home. Following this tragic event in the family's history, paranormal activity in the house increased. Barry would often play Winifred's favourite albums to remind him of his wife. These albums were old Irish songs performed by a male singer. Strangely, however, every time Barry played the songs on his record player a woman's voice could be heard singing along. He called to his children, thinking he was imagining things, but both of them confirmed his impression: they too could distinctly hear a woman singing along to the songs. The singing stopped as soon as the record was turned off, suggesting that it could be some kind of fault with the record. Barry started the record again, this time putting his ear to each speaker in turn; the only voice he could hear upon doing this was the male singer. This confirmed that the female voice appeared to be coming from elsewhere in the house. Could it have been Winifred singing along to her favourite songs?

Objects also began to move around the house of their own accord. One incident of note involved two tennis rackets. The children had been playing tennis at the local tennis courts, and, upon returning, had left their rackets on the kitchen table. Barry told them to put them away, but, children being children, they said they would do it later – and then, of course, they forgot about it and went to bed. The following morning Barry came downstairs, fully expecting to see the rackets still on the table and thinking he would have to put them away himself as usual. However, the rackets were not there – and upon checking he was pleasantly surprised to find them in the cupboard under the stairs. The children came downstairs and went into the kitchen, where Barry was making them breakfast. He told them he was surprised that they had bothered to put the tennis rackets away. The children looked bemused, and confessed that they had forgotten to do so, and were expecting to be told off. If the three people who lived in the house had not moved the objects, who had?

Similar phenomena continued throughout the latter part of the 1980s and into the 1990s. Following health problems, Barry eventually moved out of the house and into more suitable accommodation for his condition. The children were now adults and it was one of the children, Tanzie, who took over the house on Shipton Road. By 1998 Tanzie was living in the house with her husband Dave and her two children; her brother Jason was also staying with the family at the time. Paranormal activity in the home had almost died out completely, but that was to change dramatically by the end of the year.

On evening in December 1998, Tanzie was lying on the sofa in the living room; her husband was in bed, as were both of her children. She was enjoying the peace and quiet, watching television with the lights out. Then, from the corner of her eye, Tanzie noticed something moving in the room. She turned her attention from the television to the fireplace – and as she did so, she saw a grey figure manifesting from the fireplace, which then became a full-blown apparition. Unable to believe what she was seeing, Tanzie closed her eyes and opened them again. The figure was still there. Tanzie watched in shock and amazement as the grey figure floated past the sofa. It disappeared just as it reached the living-room window.

The small bedroom at the top of the stairs has been the location of various reports of paranormal activity..

The following day Tanzie received news that made her experience even more poignant. Her father had been in hospital due to his illness, and unfortunately he had passed away. Was the ghostly visitor that she had seen the night before some kind of messenger or portent of the news she was about to receive? Tanzie was unable to identify the apparition; it was too vague to say who or what she had seen. That was not to be the case almost a week later.

It was the night of 23 December 1998, the night before Barry's funeral. Thinking about her dad and his funeral the following day, Tanzie eventually fell asleep. During the night, Tanzie suddenly awoke and sat bolt upright in her bed. She looked at the foot of her bed, and saw her recently deceased father sitting in his wheelchair. Tanzie recalled that the figure she saw was a solid one and definitely her father. His facial features and attire were so vivid that she even remembered that he was wearing his glasses. Tanzie could not remember exactly what they said; she remembers that they communicated not through voice but almost 'telepathically'. She recalled the substance of the conversation was that they said goodbye to each other and that they loved each other. Barry then 'faded away'.

Tanzie and her husband travelled to Barry's funeral the following morning. The occasion was made even more sombre by Tanzie's experience of the night before and the fact that it was now Christmas Eve. On the journey home her husband made a comment out of the blue. 'We are moving house,' he said.

'What do you mean?' Tanzie replied.

'I saw you talking to your dad last night and saying goodbye. I saw you both,' he answered.

As the new millennium came around there were changes within the family structure at Shipton Road. Tanzie had remarried, her brother Jason had moved out of the house and sadly another member of the Day family had passed away. Tanzie's brother Sean had died in 2001 – and indeed an encounter with Sean was to become the third apparition to be seen in the house. Not long after Sean died, Tanzie, her husband and their daughter were sitting in the living room of the house on Shipton Road. Tanzie's four-year-old son Declan was upstairs in his bedroom, having just had a bath. As he came out of his bedroom he saw a figure near the airing cupboard, a figure he recognised. After coming down the stairs, Tanzie's son walked into the living room, smiling. Tanzie asked him why he was so cheerful, to which he replied, 'I just saw Uncle Sean on the landing.' The rest of the family were obviously startled at this revelation. Being of such a young age, Declan had no concept of what he had witnessed; he had just seen his uncle. He had no notion of what death or ghosts were. Tanzie was now aware of at least three spirits that had been seen in the house (the 'grey figure', Barry and now Sean). There was also the invisible 'entity' that had attacked her mother in the house in the 1980s. The possibility that her home was haunted by four spirits may have seemed unbelievable to her, but the situation was to become even more extraordinary.

By 2004 the paranormal activity in the house had become a regular occurrence. It seemed that whoever – or whatever – was haunting the building was trying harder to make its presence known to the family, especially to Tanzie. It may have been that

The landing area where an apparition of a man was seen one evening by a child in the house.

Tanzie was more open to the power of suggestion, which is to say that everything she was experiencing seemed 'paranormal' to her. On the other hand, maybe she was more 'sensitive' to spirits than the other people living in the house. Whichever was the case, during this period of time Tanzie had the feeling that she was never alone in the house during the day, even though nobody else was home. This often culminated with a sighting of a figure at the top of the stairs.

As the autumn of 2005 came around, further paranormal activity continued in the house. Tanzie's brother Jason was visiting. On his first evening at Shipton Road, Jason witnessed a phenomenon that is rarely seen. The family had all retired to bed for the evening, and as Jason was sleeping on the sofa during his stay he settled down for the night. As he lay on the sofa watching television, he noticed something from the corner of his eye at the foot of the stairs. Jason turned his head to get a better look, and as he watched through the open living room doors he saw a number of orbs floating in mid-air at the foot of the stairs. Orbs are believed by some to be the first stages of a spirit manifestation, but are dismissed by others as dust and insects. What is interesting in this case is that orbs are usually captured on digital photographs or seen through camcorders using night vision. They are rarely seen by the naked eye. Jason watched for a few seconds, but before he had a chance to get up and investigate further the orbs had disappeared.

The following morning Jason tried to rationalise what he had seen the previous evening, little knowing that what he would witness that night would be even more inexplicable. Jason was again sitting on the sofa in the living room watching television. It was getting late, and nearly everybody was in bed – apart from his niece Kristina, who had fallen asleep in an armchair to his right. As Jason glanced across to check on Kristina, he saw something through the open doors, and he watched in shock as a figure floated from the kitchen and across the hallway. The figure appeared to be female, though her features were hard to see. She was grey and 'not quite solid'. The woman seemed to be looking straight on towards the front door of the house, and held her hands up to her chest, almost as if they were clasped in prayer. The apparition continued its journey across the hallway and disappeared through the front door. Soon afterwards Jason woke Kristina and told her to go to bed; he mentioned nothing of what had occurred, but waited until the morning.

The next day Jason recounted the incident to his sister Tanzie. Tanzie had recently been sorting through some of their father's belongings, and what Jason had described to her had seemed familiar. Tanzie went into a cupboard and got an old tobacco tin. She opened the tin and showed Jason the inside of the lid. The tin had belonged to

The tobacco tin. Was this tin moved several times by spirits within the house, and was the lady in the photograph haunting the house herself?

their father Barry, and glued to the inside of the lid was a photo of their mother Winifred. The photo had been cut out in a way that it was the shape of her profile. The profile of the picture matched exactly that which Jason had seen the night before, even to the extent that she had her hands clasped, as if in prayer. Jason had no previous knowledge of the photograph's existence, let alone the fact that it had been cut out in such a way and put in a tin.

In the winter of the same year Tanzie fell asleep on the sofa. She woke up and realised it was just after midnight. Everybody else was in bed. She went around the ground floor of the house turning things off. She then went upstairs into the children's bedrooms, checking they were asleep and turning televisions off. Tanzie went into her bedroom and saw that her husband was also asleep. She noticed that her youngest daughter's juice cup was empty and headed back downstairs to fill it up. Tanzie got to the bottom of the stairs and turned right onto the hallway towards the kitchen door, which was wide open. The light from the streetlight outside the house was shining through the glass panel in the front door behind her so the hallway was slightly illuminated. Tanzie stopped in her tracks as she saw a figure standing in the kitchen doorway. The figure she saw was grey and looked solid: she couldn't see through it. The figure appeared to be wearing a dress, but when Tanzie looked down at the bottom of the dress she could not see any feet. She thought the figure looked female, and, though she could not see any features on the figure's face, she had a strong feeling that it was her mother. Tanzie closed her eyes and counted to ten, thinking she was imagining things. Then she opened her eyes again – and found that the figure was still looking at her. She wasn't scared: she just thought, 'Oh my God, this is real.' Tanzie closed her eyes, counted to ten and opened them three more times. Every time the figure was still there. Tanzie had the feeling that the figure was just as startled as she was, and that they had just 'happened to bump into each other'. Tanzie reached out to her left-hand side to put the hallway light on: as she did so she turned back to face the kitchen doorway. When she turned back the apparition had disappeared.

Following the sightings in 2005 physical paranormal phenomena became a regular occurrence, just as it had been in the 1980s. In 2006 bottles of cola began disappearing from the kitchen, and a computer modem that was always left in the corner of the living room went missing. The cola bottles were never seen again, but the modem was found the following day in a kitchen cupboard on the top shelf. None of the children could have reached the shelf, and neither of the adults in the house had put it in the cupboard.

Following long conversations with her brother about the paranormal activity (past and present) in the house, Tanzie decided that an investigation into what was going on there was perhaps a good idea. Tanzie's brother Jason was a founder member of the Society of Paranormal Investigation, Research, Information and Truth (SPIRIT), and as Tanzie did not want 'strangers' in her house she asked Jason and his team to investigate.

In July 2006 SPIRIT arrived at the house and set up various pieces of equipment and experiments. The team set up a trigger object in the master bedroom along with a room alarm and a voice-activated tape recorder. They then sealed off the room.

SPIRIT Paranormal Investigator Alison White investigating the activity at the house on Shipton Road. This photo was taken through the doorway where two apparitions have reportedly been seen.

With the family out of the house, the three founder members of the SPIRIT team began their night's investigation. Various unexplained sounds were heard in the house; team members experienced feelings of illness and 'being touched'. Though the team caught no solid evidence of a haunting on camera or tape, they did witness an incident that still remains unexplained: at around midnight, as the team were taking a break in the kitchen, the motion-activated room alarm went off in the sealed-off master bedroom. The team went upstairs to check the room. When they opened the door they found that the voice-activated tape recorder had also been set off, and the trigger object had been moved. The team reset the equipment and the trigger object and sealed the room once more. Later in the investigation, however, the alarm was set off again: when they investigated, they found that the trigger object had moved once again.

Having established that there may indeed be something paranormal going on in the house, the phenomena continued. In December 2006 electrical appliances began to be affected in the house. Christmas lights on the banister started running a pattern of lights independently. On the set of Christmas lights in question each sequence requires a switch to be pressed to change the pattern of lights. On the day that the lights began acting erratically the lights cycled through the different pattern of lights as if somebody was pressing the switch. This was witnessed by the only three people in the house at the time, none of whom were anywhere near the switch when the incident occurred.

The paranormal activity at the house on Shipton Road has continued well beyond 2006. The Society of Paranormal Investigation, Research, Information and Truth continue to investigate and monitor the case, and the family themselves continue to keep records of their experiences. In the four years following those covered in this book there have been many more incidents at the home. These include further sightings of 'the grey lady' and another sighting of a Victorian lady in a black mourning gown. DVD players, televisions, kettles and other electrical appliances have turned themselves on and off. Bedding and clothing has been disturbed, and at times even been moved into other rooms. As recently as February 2010, Tanzie's six-year-old daughter said that she had seen a strange woman standing at her bedroom door one evening as she was lying in bed.

Twenty-seven years, three generations and five apparitions on, the research and investigation into the case continues. With a seeming abundance of paranormal activity at the location, the question seems to be not only, 'who or what is haunting the occupants', but also, 'will the haunting ever end?'

The Haunted Factory – South Park Industrial Estate

Modern workplaces may be the last place you would expect to find a ghost, but the paranormal is all about expecting the unexpected. The South Park Industrial Estate in the Riddings area of Scunthorpe has many factory buildings, and as a consequence is home to several of the town's manufacturing and production-based employers. One such company which trades on the estate is Darby Glass, manufacturers and processors of commercial and industrial insulating glass units. The company has traded since the early 1970s, and following expansion it has spent much of that time on the industrial estate.

During the 1990s, rumours began circulating amongst staff that there may be someone or something within the building that was not 'of this earth'. Some employees on the shop floor had experienced what could have been paranormal phenomena such as 'corner of the eye' sightings of figures and feelings of unease, particularly during night shifts. As these phenomena could also be explained away by tiredness and other rational explanations, these reports were often dismissed amongst the workforce and even ridiculed by some members of staff. Those opinions changed somewhat after an unusual and unnerving encounter was experienced by an employee in the mid-1990s. In the following account the witness's name has been changed to protect his identity.

Fred had worked at the factory for a number of years, and was familiar with his surroundings and the layout of the building. He was a 'no-nonsense' type of man, and could back up his reputation with a background in power lifting and an eighteen-stone frame. One evening in the mid-1990s, Fred arrived at the factory to begin what he thought would be a 'run of the mill' night shift. At the time he worked on a machine that bent aluminium frames (which would sit in between the two panes of glass that made a sealed unit for double glazing). This machine was situated at the back of the factory behind wooden racks, thus making the machine and Fred himself quite isolated from the other employees in the factory.

A few hours into his shift, Fred was removing a frame from his machine when something caught his attention. From the corner of his eye he caught a glimpse of something moving to his right-hand side in the distance. Fred turned his head and could see the roller door in front of him, with a wall either side of it. Immediately after turning to look at the door, Fred watched as what looked like the figure of a man walked through the wall on the left-hand side. The figure had a transparent texture to it, without actually being 'see through'. Fred also noted that the man looked to be middle-aged and appeared to be from a different era, maybe from the 1950s or '60s. The man walked past the closed roller door and into the wall on the right-hand side of the door, disappearing into it. Fred was frozen for a second or two, trying to take in what he had just seen. He then dropped the frame he had been clutching in disbelief and ran to the nearest manned work station, which was a glass toughening plant. He recounted what he had seen to his colleague, who later attested to the fact that Fred was visibly shaken by his encounter. Knowing the type of man that Fred was, and that he was more than capable of 'handling himself', his workmates had no reason to doubt his word.

As the news of Fred's experience spread throughout the factory, the shop-floor staff became a little warier of working a night shift, and those that know of the phantom worker still are to this day.

The Spectral Vicar – St Paul's Church

As is the nature of the subject, many incidents of the paranormal are based on hearsay and local legend. One such story, passed down to local children, is that of the ghost of St Paul's Church in the Ashby area of Scunthorpe.

By today's standards the large red-brick church itself is relatively modern – it was built in the early twentieth century – and as a consequence the ghost that is said to haunt the building is a modern figure too. Legend has it that a former minister of the church fell to his death from the roof and that he can still be seen to this day. Even more intriguing is that he can be seen 'on demand'. It is said that if you run around the church building at midnight and look up to the roof upon completing your lap, you will see the figure of the former vicar fall from the roof in a ghostly re-enactment of his death.

Whether or not there is access to the roof of the church from inside, or if indeed a vicar ever fell to his death from the roof of the church, seems not to matter to the locals that have grown up with this legend. Many of them have taken up the challenge of running a lap of the church at midnight. They just love a good ghost story, it would seem.

St Paul's Church, Ashby, Scunthorpe

St Paul's Church roof, where a spectral vicar has been seen falling to his death.

Children Of The Plague – West Street

Scunthorpe has many local myths and legends and some are more researchable than others. One such legend incorporating paranormal activity is said to occur in the West Street area of the town. It is said that a visit to the area late at night would result in the spirits of 'ghostly' children playing 'Ring a Ring O' Roses' around you. Additional details and actual case histories are virtually non-existent, which leaves us with only theory and conjecture to work with when looking further into this legend.

The song hails from the times of the Black Death, a pandemic of bubonic plague that spread throughout Europe, peaking between 1348 and 1350 and returning periodically up until the seventeenth century. The population of England was decimated during this time, with the disease claiming an estimated 2-5 million lives. Bearing in mind

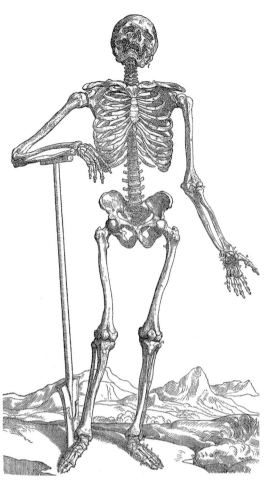

Death digs his own grave: between 30 and 60 per cent of Europe's population is estimated to have perished during the Black Death; the Great Plague of 1165-6 claimed another 100,000 souls. (Courtesy of Liam Quin, www.fromoldbooks.org)

the population of the whole country at the time was only believed to be 4-7 million people, the consequences were horrendous. The Ring a Ring O'Roses song popularised by children in the 1800s describes the symptoms, and ultimate fate, of sufferers, ending, of course, in 'we all fall down'. The children would link hands and dance around in a circle whilst they sang the song.

The relevance of this song and its history suggests that if there is indeed any credence to the legend, it may be that perhaps the area has a strong link to the period when the plague was prevalent. With a church nearby and other streets such as Chapel Street in the vicinity, it is not beyond the realms of possibility that the victims of the disease may have sought help or solace from the nearby clergy.

As with many such legends, there is usually a basis for such stories. If we cannot find the exact source of the legend then we are only left with what we can find out for ourselves and piece the rest together. One possibility is that these spirit children were victims of the plague. Another alternative is that they are from a later time in history when the song had become popularised. Whichever is the case, it seems that the most likely connection to this haunting is the plague itself. If that is indeed the case, then perhaps somehow the emotional energy connected with such a turbulent event has become trapped and manifests itself, when conditions allow, with the appearance of the spirit children.

Perhaps there may be more sightings in the future that would give paranormal investigators and researchers more solid evidence to work with.

2

Ghosts of the Surrounding Area

The Phantom Puppy – West Halten Lane – Alkborough

Not all ghostly sightings are those of menacing figures. Neither are they all of spirits that were formerly human. One such case is that of a cyclist who had a rather unusual encounter in the 1970s.

The witness was riding their bicycle along West Halten Lane in Alkborough when something suddenly ran out into their path. As they neared the cricket ground they braked suddenly, narrowly avoiding what they now knew was a small dog which had run out into the road. The cyclist watched as the puppy moved about a half a metre out of the way before vanishing on the grass verge on the other side of the road.

Was this the ghost of an unfortunate animal that had met an untimely death on this stretch of road in the past?

The Wandering Phantom – Baysgarth House Museum – Barton-Upon-Humber

Baysgarth House is the former home of the Nelthorpe family. The family were renowned in the Barton area and with the passage of time the building became a museum, eventually being transferred to the care of the CHAMP Trust in May 2004. Whilst Baysgarth House may no longer belong to the

Barton Museum and grounds.

49

Nelthorpe family, exhibits in the museum reflect the local relevance of the family and the property itself.

Local people have reported seeing a shadowy apparition within the grounds of the museum. Witnesses claim that the dark figure floats across the lawns between the car park and the museum itself. Local legend had it that a woman died trying to rescue her horse from the stables which had caught fire. It is believed that it is this unfortunate soul that now haunts the grounds. Little else is known of the entity, her identity, or whether she has been seen in the actual museum.

The Boy In The Bath – Barton Library – Barton-Upon-Humber

The building known as Providence House is now home to Barton Library. Browsing through books in the quiet ambience of a library may seen a little mundane, but the building has had a far more eventful and tragic history.

In the 1920s Providence House was an orphanage which was run by the National Children's Home organisation. During this period of history not all children in orphanages were actually orphans: some children that were placed into their care were the offspring of single parents or families that simply could not provide for them. One such child was Sidney Conway, a six-year-old boy from Holderness Road in Hull whose mother had placed him in the care of the staff at Providence House.

On Saturday 28 October 1922, Sidney and four other little boys were gathered together for their evening bath. Nursing assistant Gladys Burt sent the boys into a dressing room adjoining the bathroom and told them to undress. As the boys disrobed, Gladys went into the bathroom, put the plug in the bath and turned on the hot tap. Gladys remembered that she had forgotten one of the boys' sleeping suits and left the bathroom to go and fetch it. Three or four minutes later the sound of a piercing scream rang out through the building and Gladys rushed back to the bathroom. Upon her return she discovered young Sidney standing by the side of the bath, horribly scalded from the waist down. Gladys and the other nurses gave him what treatment they could and put him to bed.

It transpired that poor Sidney had been trying to climb over the bath to reach the other side of the room when he slipped and fell into the near boiling water. One of the other children had managed to get him out of the bath but unfortunately he was already terribly hurt. Sidney must have suffered unimaginable agony that night, as in those days there was not the medical treatment or pain relief for such injuries that we are fortunate enough to have today. Inevitably the poor child died from pain and shock four days later, on Tuesday 31 October 1922. Deputy Coroner Dr Annigson described Sidney's death as 'unfortunate'. He added that Nurse Burt was guilty of an error of judgement in leaving the boys alone before returning a verdict of accidental death.

Although little Sidney Conway's life ended here, his story continues, for there are those that believe Sidney still visits Providence House from the other side. Paranormal activity has been reported in the building for a number of years. A child's voice has been heard in the staffroom by visitors to the library who know nothing of its history, whilst others have been so sure that they can hear a child crying that they have gone in search of the source, only to find there are no children around. Other ghostly sounds that have been heard include independent reports of footsteps running down the hall, up the stairs and across the landing through a locked and alarmed glass partition.

Even more intriguing are the reports of physical paranormal phenomena. Heavy revolving bookstands are said to spin of their own accord in the library. Lights switch on by themselves in blocked off staircases, and fires are found turned on in empty rooms. There have also been several reports of self-closing fire doors swinging open on their own. Witnesses who have tried opening other doors find that they seem to be held shut by a hand grasping the handle from the other side. Staff at the library say that the activity always increases between the 28 and 31 October, and then dies back down. They also stress that they are not afraid of what they believe to be the ghost of poor Sidney. The staff believe he is not a scary or malicious spirit: to them he seems like a lonely little boy looking for a playmate, living out the life that was cruelly taken from him from the afterlife.

Barton Library, home to the ghost of Sidney Conway. (Photograph courtesy of UKPN)

Barton Library staircase. (Photograph courtesy of UKPN)

The Smoking Man – Blyborough Hill – Blyborough

Some years ago a man named Derrick had been out with a friend to the Monks Arms pub at Caenby Corner, near Hemswell. Derrick's friend left early, leaving him to try and scrounge a lift home from one of the other visitors to the pub. By the end of the evening no lift was forthcoming so he decided to walk, occasionally sticking his thumb out at passing cars in an attempt to hitch a ride. It was a nice summer's evening and he was enjoying the walk, even if it was quite a trek back to his home in the village of Blyborough. All was going well, and by the time he got to Willoughton Top he had given up trying to thumb a lift and walked the last half mile.

Just as the road rises at Blyborough Top Derrick saw someone sitting against a tree smoking a cigarette. He was a bit startled, and to ease his nervousness he called out a friendly, 'Morning!' Derrick received no response: the man just sat there smoking his cigarette. Derrick decided to approach him. Looking straight at him, he asked the man if he was all right. Still no response. By now Derrick was feeling a little bit agitated, so he nonchalantly said, 'Bye then!' and gave the man a friendly tap on his boot. To his horror, Derrick's shoe went straight through the man's foot!

At this point Derrick started to run. He only stopped running as he turned down Blyborough Hill; his house was only a few yards away, and he was out of breath, terrified and stone cold. As he got to the driveway of his house he turned to look back up the hill from where he had came – and stood in dumbstruck horror as he witnessed the figure of the man coming down the hill, with only his head and body visible to the human eye. Derek ran in to the house 'screaming like a banshee'. He recalled, 'I have never been so scared in all my life.'

The Phantom Bomber – Blyton Airfield – Blyton

RAF Blyton opened as a heavy bomber station in November 1942 and was home to 199 Squadron. Within three months the role of the station changed, 199 Squadron departed and 1662 Heavy Conversion Unit was resident for the rest of the war at the training base. Subsequently there were many crashes in the farmland around the airfield, one of which involved a HCU Halifax, crewed by Polish airmen. The bomber developed engine trouble soon after take off on 11 November 1944 from Blyton airfield. Losing altitude, the aircraft clipped a tree and crashed at East Ferry, near the River Trent. After a painstaking effort only a part of the wreckage was recovered. The airfield was very unpopular with the pilots stationed there, who believed it was filled with a bad atmosphere, and it closed in 1954. The former RAF base has since become Blyton Raceway, an off-road and stock-car racing track.

For many years following the closure of RAF Blyton the surrounding fields were haunted by a phantom airman. For some unknown reason a nearby farmhouse and the fields around it seemed to be the epicentre of the sightings.

In 1967 the remaining wreckage of the crashed bomber from 1944 was recovered. Near the pumping station known as 'The Jenny Hurne' (which is on the east side between East Stockwith and East Ferry), the fuselage of the aircraft and the remains of

The entrance to Blyton Racetrack, formerly RAF Blyton. (Photograph by Jonathan Billinger)

five Polish airmen were recovered from the River Trent. It is believed that it was this crash, which occurred twenty three years earlier, which had caused the haunting.

Unfortunately, although the airmen had now been laid to rest, the paranormal phenomena continued. One afternoon a woman received a phone call from her mother-in-law, who lives in Blyton. She told her that she had just looked out of her living-room window and saw a large 'old type' of aeroplane flying extremely low over where she lived. She said she went out of her front door to have a better look – as it was flying so low, she feared it would crash into the house opposite hers. It apparently had absolutely no sound coming from it.

A second similar sighting around the same time came from a man in his mid-thirties.

The sightings continue to this day. Maybe the men who served this country so bravely during the war want to continue to do so in the afterlife.

Feuding Phantoms – Gallows Wood – Brigg

The A18 that runs alongside Gallows Wood has had a long and chequered history. The road started life as part of a Roman road and during a period in the 1600s became a favoured haunt of highwaymen. Highwaymen preyed on travellers either operating alone, in pairs or in gangs. They would stop public stagecoaches or mail coaches and rob the occupants of their valuables. The area that would become known as Gallows Wood would provide ideal cover for the highwaymen and their horses and also footpads, who were robbers that operated on foot. Sometimes the robberies

Gallows Wood.

James I, pictured here, had a long-standing interest in the occult. He erected a gallows like this one outside Brigg to bring an end to the family feuding that had blighted life in the area. (Gallows image courtesy of Liam Quin, www.fromoldbooks.org)

would end in disaster when the victim refused to part with their valuables and the highwayman killed them, escaping into the woods with their loot.

During the seventeenth century a bitter rivalry ensued in the area between the Ross family of Melton Ross and the Tyrewitts of Kettleby. One day things came to a head when retainers from both families met whilst hunting in what is now known as Gallows Wood, three miles east of Brigg. A savage fight broke out between the Ross and Tyrewitt families and parties from both sides perished in the bloodshed.

Following this skirmish, King James I had roadside gallows erected as a reminder that any further carnage between the two families would be treated as murder. From the 1600s until the present day there have been reports of apparitions seen in Gallows Wood and on the road that is now the A18 that runs alongside it. Unexplained incidents and ghostly sightings have been regularly witnessed by staff and customers of the Gallows Wood Recovery Service located near the lay-by opposite the woods. Perhaps these apparitions are the spirits of bygone highwaymen, footpads or members of the Ross and Tyrewitt families still feuding in the afterlife.

The Lost Lady – Brigg

The term for a haunting that is specific to a location is called a residual haunting. In the case of a residual haunting, these spirits are said to be 'playing out' a past event without actually appearing to interact with the witnesses. One of the theories behind this phenomena being that the haunting is in fact a past event that has some how been 'recorded' into the fabric of the building.

There are also cases of spirits that wander freely and are sighted in various locations within a town, city or even a country. Like the residual haunting, some of these spirits are said to be 'recordings' of a past event, with no interaction with the witness to them occurring. The only difference being that, unlike the residual hauntings associated with particular buildings or areas, these ghosts appear to have a 'free will' to roam around. There are also some cases of this type of haunting where the spirit does indeed interact with an individual and even appears to have some form of independent intelligence. The following story is a case in point of this type of haunting and is made even more interesting as it also said to be time specific.

The small market town of Brigg, with a population of scarcely more than 5,000 people, is reputed to be one of the most haunted villages in the Scunthorpe area. One of the most infamous Brigg ghosts is that of an old lady seen around Christmas time. One Christmas Eve the woman left her home in Brigg to go begging for money to buy her Christmas lunch. The winter weather took a turn for the worse and as the snow and fog set in she became lost. She became more confused and disorientated in the treacherous conditions, and finally succumbed to the cold. She collapsed in the street, where she froze to death. The ghost of the poor old lady is said to appear every Christmas Eve at various locations around the village asking for directions home.

The Spectral Guest – Undisclosed Location – Brigg

Whilst visiting Scunthorpe in February 2010 I stayed in one of the town's hotels. One morning I enquired as to whether any of the staff or guests had ever reported any paranormal activity in the building. The member of staff I spoke to told me that to his knowledge nobody had ever reported any instances of paranormal phenomena in the hotel, but he did tell me all about some strange and paranormal experiences within his own home.

The staff member asked me not to mention his real name, the hotel in Scunthorpe where he worked or his full address. He did, however, give me permission to recount his story in this book.

'Tim' lives in a house in Brigg pretty much like any other in the area; he had lived there for two years without anything untoward occurring. The first instance of something paranormal happening in the house was sudden and very dramatic. Tim had returned home one evening and his wife was downstairs in the living room. He was at the foot of the stairs, about to ascend them, when a woman came down the stairs and passed him. Tim continued up the stairs, but returned to the lower floor soon afterwards. When he entered the living room he was surprised to find his wife was alone in the room. Tim asked her where her friend was, and she looked at him with a puzzled expression. Tim told her he had stood aside for a woman whom he had assumed was a friend of hers. His wife said there had been nobody in the house but her all day. Tim recounted to me that the woman he had seen had looked like a normal human being. She was a 'solid' form and dressed 'of the time'. That was why he had assumed she was just an ordinary person and not, as it had turned out, a ghostly apparition.

Soon after Tim's encounter the paranormal activity escalated. He did not see the apparition again, but other phenomena began to occur on a regular basis. Most notably for Tim, the bedroom and cupboard doors upstairs began opening and closing of their own accord. He recounted to me that these phenomena became routine for the duration of the haunting. Similarly, unexplained knocks and bangs around the house were heard by both Tim and his wife.

As with many of these stories, the paranormal activity ceased as abruptly as it had started. Suddenly the house went back to normal and no more was seen or heard of the phantom woman. Tim is convinced that what he experienced was a very real haunting; as for why it began as suddenly as it did, and why it ended, we may never know.

The Black Dog – Wrawby Road Bridge – Brigg

The Black Dog is essentially a nocturnal apparition, often said to be associated with the Devil: a 'hell hound', if you will. Examples of this are C n Annwn, Garmr and Cerberus, all of whom were in some way cited as guardians of the underworld. This association seems to be due to the scavenging habits of dogs. It is possible that the Black Dog is somehow a survival of these beliefs.

For centuries, men have told tales of a large black hell hounds with malevolent flaming eyes (or, in some variants of the legend, a single eye), usually red or green. They are described as being 'like saucers'. According to reports, the beast varies in size and stature from that of a large dog to a horse. Sometimes Black Dogs have even described as headless; at other times they seem to float on a carpet of mist.

Black Dogs and Shucks are sometimes referred to as Doom Dogs. It is said that their appearance bodes ill to the beholder, although not always. More often than not, stories tell of Black Dogs terrifying their victims, but then leaving them alone. In some cases they have supposedly appeared before close relatives of the observer become ill or die. Black Dogs are almost universally regarded as malevolent, even to the extent that their appearance was regarded as a portent of death to the witnesses themselves. A few (such as the Barghest) are even said to be directly harmful, attacking their victims on sight. Some, however, like the Gurt Dog in Somerset or the Black Dog of the Hanging Hills, are said to behave benevolently.

According to folklore, these spectres often haunt graveyards, side-roads, crossroads and dark forests. Another location associated with these ghostly beasts is bridges, as is the case with the Black Dog reported to haunt the town of Brigg. Locals warn people to stay clear of the bridge on a Saturday night to avoid an encounter with the ghostly canine.

*Wrawby Road Bridge
(left), said to be the haunt
of the Black Dog (below).*

*According to legend,
Black Shucks are thought
to haunt graveyards.
(Courtesy of Liam Quin,
www.fromoldbooks.org)*

The Haunted Vicarage – Church Of St Peter And St Paul – Caistor

The Church of St Peter and St Paul in Caistor dates back to Saxon times. It consists of a nave with aisles, a south transept, and a chancel, with a tower at the west end. There are remains of Norman work in the lower stage of the tower and an original Roman wall can be seen on the southern boundary of the Church. Over the years several repairs and renovations have taken place at the Church including the chancel, which was restored in the early 1800s and a new clock was fixed in the tower in 1854.

Having such a rich history, it would be no surprise to find out that the church is haunted, and indeed there have been reports of a ghostly monk that frequents the building. Witnesses have related hearing footsteps, banging and organ music all coming from within the church and all without an apparent 'earthly' cause. According to further reports, it is not only the church in Caistor that has a phantom occupant.

A family that lived at the vicarage adjacent to the church all reported hearing doors opening and closing when there was nobody else present in the house. Witnesses also recalled seeing a ghostly figure pass by the two large French windows in the dining room, heading toward the front door. On occasion the family claimed to have seen the apparition of a clergyman dressed in grey inside the vicarage itself.

So who could this phantom vicar be? The tale behind this haunting and the spirit who is said to be responsible for it is a tragic one indeed. During the 1800s the Revd George Watson was the vicar of Caistor. Revd Watson would travel on horseback to visit his parishioners in the outlying villages. One such parishioner was a widow whose stable he would use to rest his horse whilst he called on her. Before long rumours

St Peter's Church, Caistor.

St Peter's Church vicarage, Caistor.

began to spread amongst the villagers that Revd Watson was 'carrying on' with the widow, causing the clergyman much distress. Eventually the stress of all the conjecture became too much for the poor reverend, and in a fit of deep depression he ended his own life. A subsequent inquiry completely exonerated him of any wrongdoing, and Revd Watson was buried in the south aisle of Caistor Church.

The Ghostly Girl – Psychiatric Hospital/Workhouse – Caistor

Caistor Psychiatric Hospital was originally a workhouse, and was built in 1777. In 1800 the workhouse became a hospital for the mentally impaired, housing many patients from the age of three years old. The hospital was closed down in 1990, and the patients were relocated. The buildings were abandoned.

Following the closure of the hospital there was a fire in 2001 where many of the buildings on the site were damaged. This resulted in most of the buildings being demolished, and all that remained were the front block, the school block, the chapel and the graveyard. Sightings of apparitions and paranormal phenomena began being reported on the site, and in April 2009 PP Paranormal Investigators decided to conduct an investigation of their own at the hospital to see if they could unearth any evidence of a haunting.

The group caught what they believed to be very interesting footage on both video and in still form on digital camera. They also had intriguing audio phenomena in the shape of hearing footsteps in the chapel and also hearing a woman's voice say 'hello' in the grounds.

Following the team's investigation in April 2009, some of the buildings they investigated at the site have now been demolished. As of December 2009 all that remains of the hospital buildings is the chapel which is having new housing built around it. It will be interesting to see if the new homeowners on the site continue to see the phantom young girl with blonde hair that is said to haunt it.

The Ghost of Aubrey Clark – Railway Signal Box – Claxby

Claxby railway station was opened in 1848 and served as a part of the Lincoln to Barnetby line. Due to economic cutbacks the station closed in 1960, but the signal box on the Claxby line remained in service, even taking on some of the duties from the signal box at Market Rasen (which closed in 1981).

One evening relief signalman Aubery Clark set out to man his post in the signal box, as he had done for many years previously. Unfortunately, however, the following morning the guard of the early morning tank train found Aubery dead in the signal box. He had died of natural causes. Following his death, a colleague working in the signal box had a spate of unnerving paranormal experiences which he could only relate to spirit of Aubrey Clark still being present at the location. Another report during this time from a female motorist claimed that she saw a scooter, Aubrey Clark's mode of transport, pass across her at the railway crossing at a place where there was no road.

The signal box at Claxby was closed in 1989 and many people wondered if that would put an end to the paranormal activity at the location. This does not seem to have been the case. It was reported that the Market Rasen railway station (before its closure some years ago) regularly received the 5-5-5 bell code from the long-deserted Claxby box. This was the code for an opening signal box, which was being sent from the location, even though the building had been locked up for years. Since then, other railway workers have also reported hearing heavy breathing in the area.

Perhaps poor Aubery is not quite ready to give up his post just yet and is manning his station from the world of spirit.

The Maid and the Wench – The White Hart – Crowle

The White Hart public house is a grade II listed building which has sixteenth-century origins. At the core of the building there are sixteenth-century timber pillars and beams said to have been retrieved from Oliver Cromwell's battleships. During the reign of Charles I, he encountered problems whilst trying to collect local taxes in Crowle. To solve this problem he billeted a platoon of soldiers in the attached buildings at the back of the White Hart Inn. These men were used to 'assist' in the collection of these taxes. For these services the pub allegedly received the King's Royal Seal of approval.

Like many historic pubs, the White Hart is said to be haunted. Some visitors to the building have felt the presence of a spirit in the bar, and pictures on the walls have moved of their own accord. An apparition has been seen by staff several times when the pub is empty, leaning against one of the old posts. The ghost is believed to be a serving wench who worked at the inn during the sixteenth century. It is also said that a ghostly apparition of a maid has been seen materialising upstairs on the landing of the living quarters landing.

A paranormal investigation conducted at the White Hart in October 2009 captured some interesting light anomalies, but sadly did not capture any further evidence of the reputed haunting.

Oliver Cromwell, whose battleships were used in the construction of a Crowle pub, wrote this letter in 1645 to announce his victory at Naseby. (Image courtesy of Cate Ludlow)

The Ghost in the Iron Pot – Manor Farm – East Halton

In the 1800s it was said that that a family living in East Halton had a very peculiar belonging in their possession. The family were said to have been haunted by a monk and, more bizarrely, that they had captured the apparition. It was said that they kept the apparition prisoner in an iron pot placed in the small basement of their farmhouse home. The family believed that if the iron pot was to be removed the ghost would escape to haunt them again. Whether or not the pot remains in the basement of Manor Farm today is a mystery itself…

The Ghostly Abbot – Thornton Abbey – East Halton

Thornton Abbey was founded as a priory for the Augustinian canons in 1139 by Sir William le Gros, the Earl of Yorkshire. The priory was elevated to an abbey in 1148 because of its wealth (primarily coming from the wool trade) and influence. In 1264 the wooden structure of the abbey was rebuilt in stone and in 1382 the Abbot of Thornton was given a licence to build a gatehouse. It is believed that the licence was

Henry VIII dissolved Thornton Abbey in 1539. These two engravings depict one of the most famous scenes from Henry's reign: departing from Dover in 1520, along with the royal retinue said to number at least 5,000 members, Henry sailed to meet the King of France at the meeting known as 'the Field of Cloth of Gold'. (Image courtesy of Cate Ludlow)

Thornton Abbey Gatehouse.

granted as a result of the Peasant's Revolt of 1381, as further security against any future uprising.

The gatehouse is believed to be haunted by a man who lived, and met a gruesome end, in the abbey during this period. Thomas de Gretham was the 14th Abbot of Thornton and resided at the abbey in the 1300s. Thomas was said to have been a practitioner of the Black Arts and seeker of carnal pleasures. When his crimes were discovered he was subjected to a particularly harsh and brutal punishment: he was taken down to the monastery dungeon, where he was bricked up alive and left to die in a subterranean prison. His fate was sealed ... literally. Thornton Abbey was dissolved on 12 December 1539 by King Henry VIII and then re-founded as a college of secular cannons. Six years later the site was granted to the Bishop of Lincoln by Edward VI. During the 1600s, Oliver Cromwell attacked the gatehouse, but it proved too fortified to penetrate. Finally, Cromwell made it to the back of the gatehouse and set the wooden doors on fire. As the fire climbed up the doors, and weakened them, his men crashed through. Everyone on the inside perished. Subsequently a stately home and farmhouse were built from stone taken from the abbey church.

Today, only the threatening gatehouse, with its stone demonic faces, the barbican and a few scattered remnants of the Abbey, endure. As for those that met their end

The original fire-damaged doors at Thorton Abbey.

within the walls and grounds of the abbey, it would seem some of them may well still be with us too, even after death.

The ominous figure of Thomas de Gretham has been seen on several occasions, flitting around the grounds of Thornton Abbey, or staring with evil intent at surprised visitors who notice him standing in the dark corners of the towering gatehouse. There have also been reports of other spectral figures too, some of whom are believed to be the ghosts of the unfortunate souls who lost their lives during Cromwell's siege of the abbey in the seventeenth century.

With a history as rich and often dark as Thornton Abbey's, it seems hardly surprising that the building is believed to be one of the most haunted in the area.

The Haunted Station and the Phantom Train — Elsham

Elsham railway station was opened by the Trent, Ancholme & Grimsby Railway on 1 October 1866. Much like other TAG stations, it had staggered platforms set over a level crossing. The station was the most easterly of the TAG stations and was situated between Appleby and Barnetby railway stations. The first of two instances of paranormal activity involving the station centred on an old signal box.

Returning to the station following his shift one night, a signalman reported hearing unexplained noises during the early hours of the morning. The signalman was sitting in his signal box when he heard what sounded like a bicycle which seemed to have stopped directly outside the signal box. The signalman went to find out who his unexpected visitor could be, only to find that there was no bicycle and indeed nobody to be seen.

The most catastrophic event in the station's history led to the other instance of reported paranormal activity relating to the railway. During the 1920s a steam train was involved in an accident during foggy weather on the Elsham line near the River Ancholme Bridge. Sadly, four people died in the disaster.

It has been reported that in the same spot that the accident occurred, a large phantom steam locomotive has been seen glowing through the fog on a misty night.

Elsham railway station was formally closed by British Rail on 3 October 1993, but it would seem that service continues along its railway lines for passengers from 'the other side'.

The Ghostly Airmen – RAF Elsham Wolds – Elsham Wolds

RAF Elsham Wolds is a former Royal Air Force base located near the villages of Elsham and Barnetby, both of which are situated between Scunthorpe and Grimsby.

The base itself operated during both the First and Second World Wars, and as a consequence saw a lot of action, emotion and activity – some of which may have continued as residual paranormal energy long after the base was decommissioned. The term 'residual paranormal energy' refers to the belief that some sightings of ghosts are in fact a 'tape recording' of a past event that, under the right atmospheric conditions, can play back. The 'recordings' themselves are believed to be 'burned' into a building or area through the 'spirit energy' left behind by the person who has died, hence the term 'residual' energy. This is the type of haunting that is said to have occurred at the site during the 1950s and beyond.

Following the closure of the base as a military installation, a family moved into the flight tower and made it their home. The family soon began to witness paranormal activity. The phenomena witnessed by the family included hearing the tapping out of Morse code messages being relayed from a machine that no longer existed, and sightings of phantom airmen, dressed in RAF flying gear. The ghostly encounters were not confined to the tower itself, nor were they only the spirits of men either.

During the Second World War, the British Royal Air Force used an aircraft known as the Avro Lancaster Bomber. The bomber first saw active service in 1942 and as the aircraft was one of the main heavy bombers used by the RAF; many of them flew to and from RAF Elsham Wolds on missions. The family that lived in the old RAF tower on the site of the former airbase reported seeing a Lancaster take off from the disused runway one evening. According to the eyewitness's report, the aircraft bore the code letters PM on its fuselage.

Unfortunately, the flight tower no longer stands at the site. The tower and the family, much like the RAF base itself, are both gone. As for the airmen and the Lancaster bombers, that may be a different story. There are still occasional reports of phantom airmen at the site and even sightings of a ghostly bomber seen taking off at night over the A15 and into the skies above.

Old Jeffrey – Epworth Old Rectory – Epworth

Epworth Old Rectory is probably most famous for being the home of the founder of the Methodist Church, John Wesley. The original rectory was a thatched house which burned to the ground in 1709. John, a five-year-old boy at the time, was plucked from the fire just before the roof collapsed. The rectory was rebuilt immediately and the building is now almost as it was from the day it was reconstructed in the early eighteenth century.

John was by no means the only famous member of his family: his father Samuel, for example, was the parish priest of Epworth in the 1700s. Often unpopular with the parishioners, he was also an accomplished poet and theologian. John's younger brother was also a preacher and a poet. Indeed, he became one of the greatest hymn writers in the English language, penning such classics as 'Hark the Herald Angels Sing' during his lifetime.

The rectory has another historic claim to fame that many who may be familiar with the Wesley name may not be aware of: the building was in fact the site of the most heavily documented case of poltergeist activity in Britain, if not the world. The phenomena even occurred during the time of the Wesley's occupancy.

The haunting began in December 1716 and ended as abruptly as it began two months later in January 1717. During this period every member of the Wesley family that still resided with their father – and the household staff as well – experienced some form of the haunting. The Wesley family at home included the parents (Samuel and Susanna) and seven daughters, with a staff consisting of a manservant and a maid.

One of the first people to experience anything paranormal was a man called Robert Brown, employed as Samuel Wesley's manservant. The incident in question happened on 2 December 1716 at around 10 p.m. Robert was sitting in the dining room with one of the maids when there was a knock at the door; he dutifully opened it to find no one there. Puzzled, he returned to his seat. As he sat down again he heard another knock, this time accompanied by a soft groaning. Robert said to the maid, 'It is Mr Turpin, he used to groan so'. Once more, he opened the door and found no one there; in fact, this happened three more times. As you can imagine, both Robert and the maid were quite puzzled, but decided it was time for bed. When Robert reached the top of the stairs he saw a small hand mill turning by itself, and, to further add to his anxiety, when he finally got into his bed he heard the sound of a turkey gobbling and someone stumbling about his room.

Brown and the maid recounted their tale of continual knocking the following morning to the dairy maid, but she openly mocked the pair saying, 'what a couple of fools you are! I defy anything to fright me'. She was soon to regret her words, for that very evening, after she had finished churning and had put the butter onto a tray, she heard a loud knocking coming from the shelf where the milk was kept. She searched with a lighted candle for the source of the disturbance, but as the knocking got louder and louder she fled the room in absolute panic.

Another sceptic in the household, Betty Massy, came into the parlour one day and asked Brown if he had heard the ghost, as she thought there was no such thing. He conversed with Betty about the haunting and then knocked three times on the dining room ceiling with a reel he had in his hand. They received three knocks in reply, although there was nobody in the bed chamber above them. Betty asked Brown to repeat the exercise, so once more he knocked on the ceiling three times. On this

Right: *John Wesley, whose home was the location for the most recorded poltergeist case in history.*

Below: *Epworth Old Rectory.*

occasion the knocks they received in reply were so violent that they all but shook the house. Betty was instantly converted, and she begged Brown not knock again for fear that the entity would come downstairs to them.

Robert Brown would have further experiences throughout the haunting. These included the sounds of knocking on doors and footsteps tapping up and down the stairs in the house; he described the steps as sounding like a man in jack boots. Brown had become so perturbed by the sounds of something stumbling over his shoes, which he left by his bedside at night, that he took to leaving them downstairs. This seemed to have no affect on the phenomena, though, as the same noises occurred in his bedroom whether the shoes were there or not.

The most bizarre of Robert's experiences happened one evening in the kitchen. He was working with some tongs in his hand when he began to feel ill, and leant against the chimney. Suddenly, from behind the top of the oven, something which he described as looking like a 'white rabbit' came out into the kitchen and turned around in front of him. The apparition ran around him several times before disappearing back into the wall it had appeared from. Robert ran into the parlour, tongs still in hand, frightened out of his wits by what he had seen.

The Wesley family began to experience the paranormal activity for themselves the day after Robert Brown's first encounter.

The grounds at Epworth Old Rectory.

One evening Sukey Wesley explained to her sister Molly that she had been unnerved by some unexplained noises she had heard in the dining room the day before. As she recounted her experience, Molly seemed to make light of it; she then started to read at the table in their bedchamber. Moments later a knocking started under the table: the girls shone a candle under it, but could see no one. Then an iron casement started to rattle, the lid of a warming pan began to clatter and the latch of the bedchamber door repeatedly moved slowly up and down. The girls then heard a noise that sounded like a 'great chain falling' from the other side of the door and the windows in the room began jarring. Despite her earlier braveness, Molly was so frightened by the sudden surge of unexplained activity that she jumped into the nearest bed, still fully clothed, and pulled the covers over her head. She remained there until the morning.

A few days later, at around 5 p.m., twenty-year-old Molly Wesley had further first-hand confirmation of the haunting. Molly was reading alone in the dining room when she heard the door open and someone enter. They seemed to be wearing a long gown made of silk, as Molly could hear the rustling of the fabric as it trailed along. As they approached where she was sitting Molly looked up, but she couldn't see anyone; however, she could still hear their progress across the floor as they leisurely walked around her. She realised that running would be pointless, so she stood up, picked up her book and went to leave the room. It was only then that she discovered that, though she had heard the door open, it was closed. She hastily opened the door and ran upstairs to her mother's bedchamber, where she told her sister Emily what had occurred. Emily herself would also encounter similar phenomena: she attested to hearing what she described as 'a man wearing a loose nightgown' coming down the stairs behind her.

The girls' father, Samuel Wesley, was aware that his daughters and staff were having these strange experiences, but had had none of his own as yet. This was all about to change. Samuel ran a tight ship at the rectory, and being a strict disciplinarian he ruled his family with an iron hand. One of his house rules was that one of his daughters must wait outside his room every night until he called them to come and take his candle from the room. It was on one such night that one of his daughters, Hetty, waiting dutifully outside her father's room, heard footsteps coming down the stairs from the attic. Of her experience, Hetty wrote:

My sisters heard noises and told me of them, but I did not much believe them till one night just after the clock struck 10. I went downstairs to lock the doors, which I always do. Scarce had I got up the west stairs when I heard a noise like a person throwing down a vast coal in the middle of the kitchen. I was not much frightened but went to my sister Sukey and we together went over all the lower rooms, and there was nothing out of order. Our dog was fast asleep and our cat in the other end of the house. No sooner was I got upstairs and undressing for bed, but I heard a noise. This made me hasten to bed.

The following evening Emily Wesley waited outside her father's bedroom for the same purpose as her sister had the night before. As she left her father's room she heard a noise from the hall below. She immediately went downstairs to check on what could be making such a loud banging; as soon as she reached the hall, however, the banging started in the kitchen. As she approached the kitchen, the banging began on the outside of the kitchen door. As Emily opened the door the banging stopped – only to start again once the door was closed. Carefully, she opened the door a second time, and this time she was forced against the wall by the door she was holding. After a struggle she managed to close and lock the door. Once the door was closed the knocking started again. This time Emily ignored it and ran to her bedchamber, too scared to wake anyone. The next morning she told her mother of her terrifying experiences. Her mother replied, 'If I hear anything myself I shall know how to judge!' (She neglected to mention that she was in fact putting every incident down in letters to her son in London.)

It would not be too long before Susanna (Emily's mother) would witness the phenomena for herself. In fact, it was only a few days later: Emily and her mother heard the sound of a baby's cradle rocking violently in the nursery. When the pair investigated the commotion they found that there was nobody in the room (and no cradle either, as there had not been for several years). Susanna Wesley began to pray in an attempt to banish whatever spirit was causing the paranormal activity, but it was to no avail. This was the point at which she called upon her husband's assistance to deal with the problem.

Samuel Wesley, as was mentioned earlier, was aware of claims being made by his family and staff of the haunting in the house. He had only heard talk of it up until this point, but now he was being told directly of it by his wife he became angry. Samuel gathered the family for that evening's prayers, and as they began to pray for the King a thunderous knocking began to sound all around them. The room itself then began to rock. Samuel had at last witnessed the phenomena for himself. The interruptions to his prayers became a regular occurrence, so Samuel sought help from outside the home.

Samuel invited a fellow clergyman to join him at the rectory. The same evening Mr Hoole, a minister from the village of Haxey, took Samuel up on his invitation. When Mr Hoole arrived, Samuel told him of his family's experiences. Surprisingly, however, that evening during prayers there were no disturbances of a paranormal nature. Things were about to change, though, as Robert Brown entered the room where Samuel Wesley and Mr Hoole were conversing. 'Old Jeffrey is coming,' he announced to the men. The Wesley children had given the entity the name 'Old Jeffrey' after a man who had died in the rectory before they lived there. Brown knew he was coming because the phenomena developed a pattern, always building up in the same way. As John Wesley wrote in his account of the haunting of Epworth Old Rectory:

> It was towards the top of the house, on the outside, at the northeast corner, resembling the loud creaking of a saw, or rather that of a windmill when the body of it is turned about in order to shift the sails into the wind.

Brown was correct in his prediction, for almost as soon as he had alerted the clergymen to the forthcoming disturbances a tirade of loud knocking began. 'Come sir,' Samuel Wesley said to perplexed Mr Hoole, 'Now you shall hear it for yourself!' As the men entered the nursery the knocking transferred to the neighbouring room. When they entered the adjacent bedchamber the noises ceased and began again in the nursery. The phenomena continued in this way for some time, scaring the Wesley children (who were already in bed). Hetty Wesley was particularly frightened, so much so that she laid shaking and sweating with fear. Samuel Wesley became incensed and pulled a pistol from his belt. He pointed it at Hetty's headboard and threatened to kill the ghost if it did not cease its knocking at once. Mr Hoole was greatly alarmed by Wesley's actions and grabbed his arm shouting, 'Sir, if you are so convinced this is something supernatural, then you can not hurt it, but you give it power to hurt you!'

Wesley lowered his arm and raged at the entity: 'Thou deaf and dumb devil! Why dost thou fright these children who cannot answer for themselves? Come to me in my study, that I am a man!' The spirit answered by replicating Samuel's own knock, the one that he would use to announce his arrival at the gate. When the entity did this, by banging on the headboard, it knocked so hard it almost broke it. The room then fell silent.

It would seem that Old Jeffrey took Samuel up on his challenge the very next evening. Wesley went to his study. He was the only person in the house with a key to the room, and as he was about to unlock the door it swung open with such force that it almost knocked him to the ground. With that, the knocking began again, going from one wall of the study to another and eventually manifesting in the adjoining room (where Nancy Wesley was at the time). Upon entering the room, Samuel remarked to his daughter, 'These spirits love darkness', and he put out the candle which he was carrying; 'Now perhaps it will speak.' Samuel received no vocal response from the entity, just the continuance of the knocking. He spoke once more to his daughter, 'Nancy, two Christians are an over match for the Devil. Go downstairs. It may be when I am alone he will have the courage to speak'. Nancy did as her father had requested and went downstairs.

The upper floors of the rectory are said to be haunted by the ghost of Old Jeffrey.

The Wesleys believed that the Devil was at work in the haunting of the rectory. This vision of the Devil (showing a knight riding past Death whilst the Devil looks on) was drawn by Albrecht Dürer in the sixteenth century. (Courtesy of Liam Quin, www. fromoldbooks.org)

Samuel and his wife Susanna Wesley had brought nineteen children into this world, of which only ten had survived. One of the unfortunate children who had passed away was also called Samuel. With this in mind, and left on his own to talk to the spirit, Wesley said aloud, 'If thou art the spirit of my son Samuel, I pray you knock three times and no more'. He was answered with silence.

From here on it seemed that entity now diverted its attention from the rest of the family: it was now fully focused on Samuel himself. The knocking followed him day and night, throughout the whole of the house. The only warning he received before any paranormal phenomena in the rectory was the whining of the family's dog, which always came seconds before any event. Samuel's son John Wesley remarks in his account:

My father was thrice pushed by an invisible power, once against the corner of his bed, then against the door of the matted chamber, a third time against his study door. His dog always gave warning by running whining towards him, though he no longer barked at it as he did the first time.

Things escalated rapidly from this point, and all sorts of strange things began to happen around the house. It was around this time that the ghost made its first physical appearance to Samuel's wife Susanna. She described it as being 'like a badger but without a head', and she saw it running under her daughter Emily's skirts. It continued to make itself known to the household, running continually up and down the stairs. Door latches would lift by themselves: when the children tried to hold them down they found it could not be done, as if an unseen hand was holding them up. It was Hetty Wesley that seemed the most upset by the ghost. Her fear was so great that she was having trouble sleeping and even breathing at times. Her father Samuel Wesley continued to be the most affected by Old Jeffrey. The spirit would constantly disturb him during his prayers and Samuel would follow the sounds from room to room. He took to spending long periods of time alone in his study trying to speak with the presence: the only answers he ever got were the sounds of a small animal squeaking.

As the paranormal activity continued into its second month, the story of the haunting was beginning to spread around Epworth and beyond. Many of his parishioners tried to reason with Samuel Wesley, asking him to leave the rectory – if not for his own sake then for that of his family. He refused, saying, 'No! Let the Devil run from me! I will never run from the Devil!'

At this point, however, Samuel Wesley wrote to his eldest son (also named Samuel) in London, asking him to return home. Before Samuel could make his travel arrangements he received a second missive from his father telling him that all had returned to normal and peace once again reigned in the parsonage. The disturbances had ceased as suddenly as they had begun.

The case was documented by most of the family and staff. For the whole two months and beyond, documentary evidence was kept by several witnesses. This included letters, diaries and eyewitness testimonials. Of its time, and even now, the Epworth poltergeist case remains one of the best documented paranormal cases in history. So who or what was haunting the Wesley family?

Little was known of the poltergeist phenomena in the eighteenth century, so it is understandable that the Wesleys would have had little idea about what could be causing the strange phenomena. Nearly 300 years and several cases later, we have a little more knowledge on the subject. Most poltergeist cases occur in households where there is a child reaching puberty, usually a girl. Other common factors in such cases include households that are predominantly religious, where the parents are strict and also sometimes where the children have problems such as Tourette's Syndrome or Attention Deficit Disorder. As the Wesley household was indeed a very religious one and contained nine girls at the time of the haunting, it may be quite feasible that this could have been a genuine poltergeist case. What paranormal investigators do not yet know is whether poltergeist activity is psychokinetic energy that is being emitted from the child whom the phenomena is centred around, or whether it is an outside entity that is using that child's energy to manifest itself. It is possible that there are indeed logical explanations for the Epworth poltergeist case. The family and staff could have misinterpreted normal occurrences, or have even made the whole thing up. On the other hand, perhaps the events were really paranormal. Maybe the psychokinetic energy causing the phenomena was coming from Molly or Hetty Wesley. It could even be the case that the spirit of Old Jeffrey used the energy of the children and the household itself to manifest himself. Indeed he may even now be lying in wait at Epworth Old Rectory until the right people and conditions come along again and he can once again make himself known.

The Woman in Black – Low Melwood Farm – Epworth

Between 1395 and 1396, Thomas Mowbray (who would later become Duke of Norfolk) founded a Carthusian priory in Melwood Park near Epworth. On the site of the monastery at Low Melwood, in Epworth, stood a chapel dedicated to the Virgin Mary; it had long been called the 'Priory in the Wood'. The priory remained in the monk's hands until Royal Commissioners arrived to take the surrender of the house on 18 June 1538. Following a failed effort to force the Carthusian monks to assent to the King's will regarding the oath of supremacy, Augustine Webster, prior of Melwood, was executed, and the priory was signed over to the Commissioners.

This image, from Grose's Antiquities, *shows all the orders of the monastries: a Carthusian monk, such as would have lived at Low Melwood, can be seen in the centre of the image (standing fifth from the left, with white robes and hood up). (Courtesy of Liam Quin, www.fromoldbooks.org)*

Few traces of the priory now remain; in its place stands Low Melwood Farm, though it would appear that not all the traces of the priory's history have vanished with time.

As far back as the 1800s there have been reported sightings of a phantom lady wearing a black silken gown wandering around the site of the old priory. Although her identity is unknown, it is believed she had some kind of connection to the building.

Phantoms of The Old Hall – Gainsborough Old Hall – Gainsborough

The land that Gainsborough Old Hall was built on is the site of a former castle which was attacked by an invading army led by King Sweyn from Denmark in the eleventh century. Sweyne made his winter camp in Gainsborough, where he received the submission of Eorl Uhtred and all of Northumbria, as well as the people of Lindsey and of the Five Boroughs. Before Christmas 1013 all of England north of Watling Street had surrendered to Sweyne, and in 1014 Sweyne went to Bury St Edmunds to demand tribute payment. The people refused and prayed to St Edmund for help. Shortly after, at his camp in Gainsborough, Sweyne died. It is said that St Edmund appeared to him and ran him through with a lance. Sweyne supposedly shouted, 'Help! Help! St Edmund has come to kill me!' When his men arrived they found him dead, covered in his own blood. However, he actually died after falling from his horse!

Local legend has it that the sounds of the dying leader of the Danish warriors can still be heard on occasion today.

The paranormal activity seems to have carried through to the current building that now stands on those grounds. Gainsborough Old Hall is over 500 years old and one of the best preserved medieval manor houses in England.

The hall was built by Sir Thomas Burgh around 1460. The Burghs were rich, flamboyant and powerful people. Gainsborough Old Hall was not only their home, but also a demonstration of their wealth and importance. Architecturally it has changed very little over the years.

It is principally a timber-framed building, giving it its characteristic 'striped' or 'black and white' appearance. On the north-east corner is a brick tower which has a fifty-nine step climb to the top.

The tower room itself has a grisly history: the story goes that Thomas Burgh's daughter Elizabeth fell in love with a servant or poor soldier. As punishment for being in love with somebody 'beneath her', she was locked in a room where she starved to death. There have been several reported sightings of the ghost of poor Elizabeth in the room where she met her cruel fate.

Between the 1930s and '40s the caretaker of the hall used to tell a tale of arriving at work in the morning to find some of the portraits in the building had been turned completely upside down. He would then correct this anomaly and go about his daily routine before going home. Upon returning to work the following day he would be met once again by the upside-down portraits. This unexplained occurrence would be a regular feature of his working life at the Old Hall.

Another spirit reported in the building is that of a shadowy form of a woman seen passing through walls on the site. There have also been reports of unexplained noises, voices and 'cold spots' at this location.

A recent paranormal event held at the Old Hall may have unearthed another ghost. During a paranormal investigative experience in 2009 hosted by UK Paranormal Network, members of the team reported a strange sighting. UKPN founder Sam Brown was following fellow founder Gary Brown into the kitchen during the initial group walk around. She turned to look into the great hall to make sure everyone had followed Gary and saw a figure – which she assumed was fellow investigator Paul – walking away from the group. Sam set off to follow him. Team member Kaz had also seen someone walking away and also took the route towards the shop where she thought they had gone. The two soon realised no one was there, and that Paul was with the rest of the group in the kitchen. On reflection, Sam describes the figure she saw as being a 'well-built male dressed in dark clothing'. She clearly saw him turn as he walked away from the group and head towards the far end of the Great Hall before turning into an alcove.

Ghosts of the Past – Old Nick Theatre – Gainsborough

The Old Nick Theatre, a grade II listed building in the heart of Gainsborough, started its life far back in Victorian times as the town's police station and courthouse. In 1979 the property was acquired by the Gainsborough Theatrical Co. Patron Douglas Parkinson leased the venue to the company for a nominal rent, and they transformed the premises to create a bar, coffee room, costume/props stores and a unique fifty-five-seater 'theatre in the round' where the courtroom had been. Downstairs, the new box office replaces the original reception rooms and, still hidden from view, are the original police cells, some complete and still decorated with acerbic graffiti from previous 'residents'. The newly rechristened Old Nick Theatre opened to the public in 1980. Douglas Parkinson became the company's first Honorary President, enjoying the results of his generosity until he died in 1993, paying GTC the ultimate compliment by leaving them the Old Nick building in his will.

It is claimed that the Old Nick is a very actively haunted location. Visitors and paranormal investigators alike have reported an uneasy feeling of being watched and followed, hearing phantom voices and footsteps, and seeing orbs, light anomalies and more. Paranormal investigation teams and event companies regularly visit the place to further explore the alleged phenomena. Experiments including glass divination, séances and the use of psychic mediums at the Old Nick have all yielded interesting results. Many of those that have explored the possibilities that the former courthouse may be haunted believe that the restless spirits may be those of the men who enforced the law or passed sentence on the condemned within its walls. Similarly, the identities of the more malicious entities in the old police station are alleged to be the ghosts of the criminals that once inhabited its cells.

The Village That Isn't – Abandoned Medieval Village – Gainsthorpe

In the seventeenth century a village once stood midway between what are now known as Lincoln and Winteringham. The thriving village was known as Gainsthorpe and had over 100 houses on its land. Gainsthorpe became a refuge for thieves and robbers who waylaid travellers on the old road that past the village. The crimes became so problematic that the road, which once followed the straight line of Roman Ermine Street, was adjusted to take an unexpected bend so as to detour Gainsthorpe.

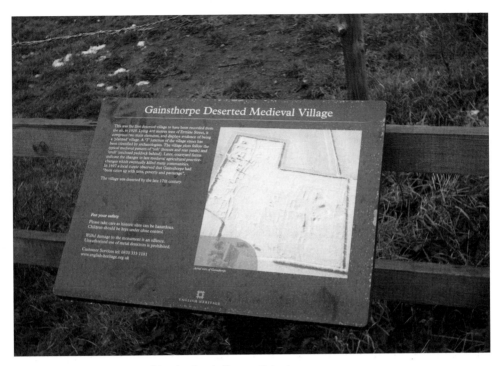

The sign indicating the location of the abandoned village at Gainsthorpe.

The abandoned medieval village of Gainsthorpe.

People from the neighbouring villages of Kirton Manton, Scawby, Cleatham and Hibaldstow had been dealing with this problem for some time during the 1600s, and eventually they decided to take matters into their own hands once and for all. They made their way to Gainsthorpe *en masse* and laid waste to the village, leaving it in ruins and executing the robbers. The victorious mob then threw the lifeless bodies of the slain down a well. Gainsthorpe was immediately abandoned by the remaining residents and became a ghost town.

Now all that remains is a solitary farm in fields to the west of the modern A15 marking the spot where this once thriving village stood. The fields remain preserved as English Heritage land and a plaque alerts visitors to the significance of what once stood there. The plaque, however, does not alert people to the fact that the site is allegedly haunted.

Witnesses have reported seeing phantom figures dressed in seventeenth-century clothing crossing the field on numerous occasions. The ghosts then disappear at what is believed to be the site of the well.

The Phantom Flyers — Raf Hemswell — Hemswell Cliff

RAF Hemswell was built in the 1930s to a very high standard and was one of a number of permanent bases built to accommodate the then rapidly expanding RAF. On 31 December 1936, Hemswell was opened as one of the first airfields within No. 5 Group of the newly formed Bomber Command.

144 Squadron arrived on 9 February, and 61 Squadron on 8 March 1937, equipped with Avro Anson and Hawker Audax aircraft. Bristol Blenheims replaced these by January 1938 and just a month later one of many tragedies to occur at the base happened. On 10 February 1938, P/O Richard Maxwell crashed the aircraft he was piloting at the Hemswell airfield. Maxwell and Corporal David Wissett were killed and the other crew member, A/C 1st Class Whitfield Dodds, was injured. By 20 March the following year the base was completely re-equipped with Handley Page Hampden bombers. Hemswell's Hampdens are credited with being the first Bomber Command aircraft to drop bombs on German soil.

A female ambulance driver named Joan, who was stationed at RAF Hemswell during wartime, witnessed a number of accidents at the base. One memory in particular is of a crash which occurred at the 170 hangar when a 170 squadron plane crashed. The pilot was badly injured; he died on the way to hospital in the ambulance. Joan had to take the MO a cup of tea, but she couldn't face going into the medical office so slid the tea along the floor. She vividly remembers seeing the bodies laid out, and how she cried that day.

The last hostile operation during the Second World War from Hemswell was on 25 April 1945, the target being the SS Barracks at Berchtesgaden. From 29 April final war operations were of a more humane nature, when 150 & 170 Squadrons took part in Operation Manna, dropping food to the starving Dutch people prior to final surrender on VE Day, 8 May 1945. From then until their disbandment in November

1945, 150 and 170 Squadrons used their Lancasters, firstly to transport ex-POWs back to the UK, and then to collect long-serving 8th Army men from Italy to well-earned leave in the UK.

The much longer Cold War brought a new purpose to the base. By 1959 Hemswell was equipped with Douglas Thor Missiles, and it became the lead station of a group of five missile sites. They were all on full alert, twenty-four hours a day, 365 days a year. At that time, RAF Hemswell had a large contingent of Americans who partnered their RAF counterparts and lived among the personnel on the station. After the Thor missiles were withdrawn in 1963, the Americans left and the missiles were returned to the USA, where most of them were used in the US Space Programme.

Following on from this, and an ill-fated training course on TSR2 avionics systems that was suddenly cancelled, the final RAF use of the base was as No. 1 Recruit Training School.

In 1967, the RAF switched off the lights, closed the gates and the base entered a very unhappy period; its handsome buildings were to be sadly neglected for many years. Some years later, a group of entrepreneurs decided to try to rescue the site and turn it into a trading estate. Although not preserved as a museum, the old road layout has been retained and most of the buildings have been restored for various new uses.

One of the first reports of a haunting relating to the 'old air base' occurred just eleven years after the RAF had left the site. In 1978 a man was driving home when he pulled over at the former RAF base for a rest. He got out of his car to stretch his legs when he heard music in the distance. He described the music as 'The Missouri Waltz', a song which was popular during the Second World War. Suddenly the music stopped, and the man heard the sound of a lorry starting up and then coming to a halt closer to where he stood. He was unnerved by this experience, but things quickly became more bizarre as the man began to hear loud talking and laughing. Unable to see any possible source for the sounds he was hearing, the shaken man hastily jumped back in his car and drove home as quickly as he could.

Interestingly, in January 2009 a group of paranormal investigators carrying out research at the location also reported hearing music, this time from one of the hangars. As they approached the building the music stopped. The team also recorded capturing interesting light anomalies on their digital cameras, and what they claim to be the sound of a male voice saying 'walk this way' on a digital voice recorder.

The paranormal phenomena in and around the area of the base does not stop there. Motorists have driven past RAF Hemswell and reported seeing airfield landing lights illuminating the skies, only the runways are now ploughed fields. One particular witness described driving along the road to Scunthorpe on a section of road that was in total darkness. The witness stopped the car to let their children 'experience the darkness' when they noticed an aircraft circling the airfield. The strange thing was there was no engine noise and the aircraft flew in absolute silence. The driver later found out that they had stopped on a cliff top and as that section of the A15 is lit up, and including the fact that most of the north Nottinghamshire and South Yorkshire valleys are on the western side of the road, it would have required a major power cut throughout the area for total darkness to have ensued there that night.

Within the site of the former base itself even more strange reports have occurred. One witness recalled staying in a nearby hotel where some electrical construction workers were also residing. The workers were carrying out some work at the site and were very reluctant to work there after dark. The witness recalled that one evening the workers returned from the base as usual, packed their bags and left. Their reason for doing so was imparted to the witness as they left the hotel still pale and shaking. One of the workers simply said they had had an 'experience' in one of the old hangars.

Whilst looking around one of the old hangers, another person had a strange experience (which was also witnessed by their father). As father and child browsed around the furniture and equipment that was for sale in the building they heard a phone ringing. The phone continued to ring for such a length of time that the father even declared vocally that he wished somebody would answer it. Much later they were to find out that there was no phone in the hangar and that the constant ringing of a 'ghostly phone' is one of the many reported paranormal phenomena on the site.

There are two very unnerving apparitions that are frequently reported at the former RAF Hemswell Airfield. Firstly, there is the ghost of an engineer who lost his arm in machinery whilst working at the base. He is seen staggering around the site screaming and clutching at his mutilated limb. Equally disturbing is the phantom pilot who crash-landed at the site: he is seen running down the old runway with his clothing still ablaze. Perhaps this second spirit is P/O Maxwell or Cpl Wissett, doomed to relive that tragic day in February 1938 forever.

The phantom pilot.
(Illustration by Jason Day)

The Vanishing Passenger — Keadby

The term 'Road Ghost' is often used when referring to a phantom hitch-hiker, and is a whole sub-genre of hauntings within itself. A common belief is that such lost souls are trying to complete a journey; perhaps they have some unfinished business, and will continue to repeat that journey until they complete their task.

One such road ghost was encountered by a taxi driver in Keadby in 2001. The taxi driver was hailed by a young girl at a lay-by near Keadby Bridge. The girl flagged the taxi and the driver pulled into the lay-by. The girl got into the back of the cab and asked the driver to drop her off near the football ground. As is typical with these cases, the driver did not think anything unusual of his passenger: there was nothing strange about her appearance or demeanour. They did not talk as they drove, but that was nothing new. Sometimes people are not very talkative, and just want to get to where they are going. As the driver reached his destination he came to a halt and stopped his meter. A chill ran down his spine as he turned to ask the girl for the fare, for he realised she had vanished. At no point during the journey had he seen the interior light of the taxi come on or heard a door open or close. There was no logical explanation for how the girl had exited the vehicle without him knowing. She had simply disappeared.

The lay-by in Keadby where a taxi driver picked up a ghostly passenger.

The Ghosts of Squadron 33 – Kirton in Lindsey

The Royal Flying Corps (later to become the Royal Air Force) airfield in Kirton in Lindsey was used during the First World War from December 1916 to June 1919. The airfield was home to detachments of 33 Squadron from their nearby Gainsborough base.

No. 33 Squadron was formed from part of 12 Squadron at Filton on 12 January 1916. For the remainder of the First World War the squadron was employed in the Home Defence role in Lincolnshire, guarding against German airship raids against northern England. The squadron's flights were spread over three separate stations: RAF Scampton (A Flight), RAF Kirton in Lindsey (B Flight) and RAF Elsham Wolds (C Flight). Equipped with the Bristol Fighters and Avro 504s, 33 Squadron did not destroy any enemy airships, despite a number of interceptions; it was disbanded in June 1919.

Between 1916 and 1919, RAF Kirton in Lindsey saw its fair share of action and tragedy. On the night of 4/5 August 1918, Lt Frank Benitz (a member of 33 Squadron based at Kirton) had been on patrol in a Bristol Fighter, looking for German bombers which were carrying out a raid. On landing he misjudged his height in the dark and crashed. He was killed on impact (and, because he had been on a patrol, listed as killed

The former home of Squadron 33, RAF Kirton in Lindsey.

in battle), and his observer, Second-Lieutenant H.L. Williams, was seriously injured. The base was also the victim of a direct hit during the Battle of Britain. Barrack Block 37 was destroyed, and a number of French pilots that were housed there were killed.

With the end of the war, the airfield was returned to agricultural use, but reports would suggest that some of the pilots who gave their lives at the base may be spending their afterlives there.

Eerie garbled conversations spoken in French, and the phantom screams of men in pain, have been heard in the area of what was Barrack Block 37. These ghostly voices are said to be those of the pilots who lost their lives in the air raid. Some witnesses have also reported seeing the apparition of a man, dressed in a pilot's uniform, lurking by an old hanger. Could this be the ghost of Lt Benitz, buried in a nearby graveyard in Gainsborough, trying to make his way back to base after his ill-fated flight?

The Low Road Phantom – Kirton in Lindsey

Mystery and intrigue still surround the sighting of a ghost on Low Road just outside of Kirton Lindsey.

The most often repeated story of an encounter with the spirit is that of two men who were cycling back home from Kirton along the road to Grayingham. Whilst making their way home one evening, both cyclists observed the figure of a man floating across their path. No doubt, following their experience, the men made their way back home in record time! The same spectre has been sighted on several occasions since this report, and his identity is said to be that of a man who met an untimely death more than a century and a half ago.

On a bleak night in December 1847, thirty-year-old farmer Charles Copeman was making his way around several drinking establishments in Kirton. During his pub crawl, Copeman visited such hostelries as the Greyhound, the Red Lion and the George, the latter of which is the only pub that is still open today.

At some point in the evening Copeman crossed paths with twenty-two-year-old Joseph Travis, a cabinet-maker, of Manor Farm on Dunstan Hill, Kirton, a man known to be in debt to several people. Reports of the evening's events suggest that Copeman was seen to be flashing around gold sovereigns, something that had not gone unnoticed to the opportunist Travis. Travis kept his eye on Copeman's movements (and no doubt his purse too) and followed him around the local pubs, 'befriending' him along the way. At the conclusion of the night's drinking, Copeman headed along Low Road towards Grayingham and what would ultimately be home once he reached Blyborough. Unfortunately, however, Copeman never made it home, as at some point on his journey along Low Road his new acquaintance Joseph Travis robbed and murdered him. He wanted to get hold of the money to pay off some of his debts.

The view of the local people in the area is that the ghost that the two cyclists reported seeing on Low Road, and indeed the many sightings of the apparition thereafter, is that of Charles Copeman, still trying to make his way home after that fateful night more than 160 years ago.

The Haunted Tower – All Saint's Church – Laughton

All Saints' Church in Laughton is a medieval building, with Norman arches and a rich Victorian interior and chancel. The most interesting feature of the building, from a paranormal point of view, is not what the building is made up of, but what may lie within it.

Since the 1970s there have been reports of unearthly footsteps emanating from the church with no apparent source for the sounds. Witnesses alone in the church have reportedly heard not just one set but whole groups of ghostly footsteps coming down the stairs from the church tower.

The most compelling account of this phenomenon came from a workman in the 1970s who was working in the church repairing the tower. The builder heard the sound of footsteps coming up the stairs and looked around, fully expecting to see somebody on the stairway. There was nobody there. Believing he may have misheard or imagined the noise, he once again set about his work – and once more he heard the sound of feet on the tower stairs. On inspection, as before, there was nobody to be seen anywhere on or near the stairway. After twice encountering the phenomena for himself, the builder had heard enough: he downed his tools and left the church, flatly refusing to work alone in the haunted tower.

The Shaking Gravestone – Laughton Woods

In the early 1800s a man by the name of Richard Rainsforth from East Ferry made his living as a fellmonger on Laughton Common. The job entailed skinning animal carcasses and selling the hides, and so what he earned was very much dependant on the mortality rate of the cattle. Hemp growing was very much a part of the agricultural year in Laughton and Scotton, and as a part of the process of cultivating hemp poisonous hemp water could be found in the hemp pits.

Richard saw an opportunity to earn a little extra money during 'lean periods', and embarked on the bright idea of giving the cattle on the Common the hemp water to make them sick and, ultimately, cause them to perish (thus maximising his income). Local farmers eventually realised what Richard was up to and sought vengeance. To evade the law Richard fled to a barn at East Ferry, and rather than be captured he hanged himself. As a suicide he couldn't be buried in consecrated ground, so his body was taken to Laughton Common and laid to rest there.

A newspaper report from 1901 tells how 'Old Rainsforth at the Crossroads has a wire fence and a drain around him, evergreen on both sides of him'.

Another, much later, newspaper report is even more intriguing. The report, from 1977, is entitled 'Gravestone that shakes at Midnight', and reads: 'Locals say if you stand on the gravestone at midnight it starts shaking and then Dickie's ghost gets up and roams the Common'. The article goes on to quote former head keeper of the Laughton Estates Mr Frank Coates (eighty-three), who says, 'I know the legend from my youth. He hung himself in Read's barn.' Mrs Winefred Needham (seventy) of Linden Cottage, Wildsworth was also interviewed and said that the barn was owned by the Ellis family when Dickie committed suicide. She said Mr Daniel Ellis, the farmer, cut Dickie down and kept the rope, which she remembered seeing when she was younger. Mrs Needham said Danny Ellis' granddaughter threw the rope out, considering it unlucky.

Church registers show that Richard Rainsforth and his wife Lucy had a daughter, Ann, baptised in August 1758. In August 1752 a Richard Rainsforth and wife Ann had a son, Thomas. Were there two Richard Rainsforths or did the one remarry? Whatever the case may be, Richard Rainsforth is buried in a grave in what is now known as Laughton Woods. So if you happen to be walking there one evening, be sure not to stand on his gravestone at midnight – for if you do, be warned: you may come across the ghost of 'Old Dickie'.

The Playful Children – Regent Terrace – New Holland

The village of New Holland is five miles east from Barton-upon-Humber. The village developed due to the increasing trade from coaches taking travellers to the ferry that crossed the River Humber from New Holland to Hull in the 1830s, and also the arrival in 1848 of the Manchester, Sheffield and Lincolnshire Railway. The arrival of the railway resulted in a dock and pier being built, making transfer from the railway to the steamers easier. Trains continued using the New Holland pier until 1981 and the opening of the Humber Bridge.

Most of the homes in New Holland were terraced 'two up two down's resided in by local railway workers and those associated with the ferry terminal.

The demise of the ferry after the Humber Bridge was built saw many homes sold off very cheaply, and the building plots used to build newer homes. However, some of the old housing remained. Regent Terrace was a set of ten homes and two shops, all joined by loft space and with interior modernisation only. Most of them still held the original coal fires and chimney stacks.

Number 8 was purchased by Sam Brown in January 2004. It was in a sorry state and required a new kitchen, bathroom, heating, doors and windows. Due to the volume of work being carried out, Sam and her family did not move in until April that year.

From the day the family moved in, they found the house to be cold and dark. Visitors to the home would describe it as having a 'stifling atmosphere'. However, Sam and her three children settled in fairly quickly and made it their home. Sam was working full-time and her children were either at school or with childminders. Due to her busy lifestyle, Sam and her children would often only be home at night and the occasional weekend. When they were in the house Sam would regularly wake to the sounds of one of the children crying, saying they had seen a hand come from under their bed. Initially Sam put it down to 'night terrors' and paid the incidents little attention.

Over the next two years Sam recalled many strange incidents in the home. The handle on her bedroom door was a small spherical wooden knob. She would often come home to find it had fallen off and was at the bottom of the stairs. This became such a regular event that she eventually just left the handle off rather than having to keep fixing it back on. Sam also began noticing unusual noises at the house, such as bangs, taps and shuffling noises, as if someone was walking in socks across a wooden floor. More bizarrely, Sam began hearing the sound of what she described as 'the flapping of curtains in the wind' coming from the loft. At the time she put the noises down to living in a terraced house and the possibility of sound travelling through from the neighbours' properties.

In August 2006 Gary (Sam's husband) moved into the house. If Sam thought the things that she had experienced so far could be explained, what occurred whilst the couple were redecorating certainly made her think again.

The layout of the first floor of the house meant that as you went up the stairs the master bedroom was directly on the left and the children's rooms were down an L-shaped corridor. The door to Sam's eldest son's room was on the right, the first side of the 'L', and the younger two sons' room was at the end of the 'L'. Sam was painting the youngest children's bedroom whilst Gary was at work and the children were at school. Suddenly, she heard banging coming from down the corridor. She stepped off the ladder and opened the bedroom door to see a DVD case lying at the corner of the 'L'. Sam tried to recall if it had been there before she had entered the bedroom. As she did so, she heard another three bangs and saw another DVD 'fly' down the corridor and land near the one already on the floor. She walked up the hallway and peered around the corner, expecting to see her husband home from work early and playing pranks on her. As she reached the corner she saw another two DVDs on the floor near the bookshelf containing the rest of the movies. Neither Gary, nor anybody else, was home.

Another incident that followed shortly afterwards was witnessed by the whole family. The stairs ran along the back wall of the living room and the sofa was situated against the stairs. As the family were watching television one evening they heard extremely loud banging, as if someone was falling down the stairs. The thudding noise as something hit each step caused Sam to instantly jump up, thinking it was one of the children. It was at this point that she realised they were all in the living room with her and Gary: there was nobody upstairs. They looked high and low for the cause of the disturbance. They checked boxes that may have fallen from shelves, pictures that may have fallen from walls – they even checked on neighbours and in the loft in case they were mistaken as to where the sound had come from, but they could find no logical explanation.

Extended family members and friends who visited the house also began to experience unusual activity. When visitors stayed over at the house they usually slept in the youngest boy's room. Following their stay they would often ask Sam and Gary what they were doing in the corridor the previous evening, even suggesting they were looking in on them in the room. They would then explain to their surprised visitors that they had no need to go into that part of the house as the bathroom was downstairs and the master bedroom was at the top of the stairs.

Sam and Gary's children began witnessing paranormal activity themselves. In fact, it was one of the children who first saw an apparition in the house. One afternoon their youngest son had headed upstairs. Almost immediately Sam heard a scream, and her son ran back down the stairs, shaking and crying. Through his tears he told Sam, 'There's a boy, there's a boy and he looked at me.' She calmed him down and asked him exactly where he had seen this 'boy'. He explained he had turned into the corridor and seen a hand on the edge of the door, which was slightly ajar. Suddenly a boy's face popped around the door and looked straight at him. Her son refused to accompany Sam upstairs so she went to investigate alone. There was no one up there. He refused to go upstairs alone after his experience.

One evening the couple's eldest son woke up screaming. Sam tried to get into his room to calm him down, but it felt like there was some sort of force keeping her from opening the door. Eventually she was able to enter the bedroom and calm him down. Her son said a hand had come from under his bed and grabbed him. The following morning he didn't remember the incident.

Who or what was haunting the house on Regent Terrace? Quite often Sam and Gary would be sitting watching television when a child would dart from the doorway and run behind their other sofa. When they checked, however, it wasn't one of their children. Sam recalls that on one occasion she saw the boy dressed in shorts, braces and a white shirt with a flat cap.

Sam and Gary became friendly with the son of the couple who had lived in the house prior to them owning it. One day Sam was visiting the shop that the couple now ran when the woman said to her, 'You have two children living in your home.'

'No, I have three children,' Sam replied.

'You have an extra two children living there then?' The woman responded.

Sam asked her what she meant, and the woman simply said, 'They'll make themselves known if they haven't already.'

The family became accustomed to the paranormal activity going on. They didn't usually admit it to people, as they were well-respected paranormal investigators and Sam was a psychologist. The couple felt that if they admitted to what was happening in their home, it would affect their reputation and business.

Sam and Gary did discuss the events with their neighbours though, and were informed that paranormal activity had been happening for many years within three of the homes on the street. The residents of one told the Browns of many unexplained incidents. They even reported seeing a male figure walk through the wall heading towards the next house. They also reported hearing noises in the loft space; jewellery regularly went missing, only to reappear months later. They were convinced that the figure they had seen was the spirit of a railway worker, and they had consulted a local psychic, who had described the apparition as a young man with no ill feelings.

Sam, Gary and the children moved out of the house in December 2009 due to Sam's ill health. The family still held the keys to the house as they had yet to complete a sale. The plan was to move out, sell off the furniture they no longer wanted, clean the house up and then sell it. They checked on the house almost everyday initially, then once or twice a week. They decided not to renew their buildings and contents insurance when it ran out in December, knowing they would be selling the house within a few months.

In January 2010 Sam and Gary's children came home from school saying they had been told the house on Regent's Terrace had burnt down in a fire the night before. Sam checked the local news and there was indeed a report saying that a serious house fire in New Holland had destroyed five houses. Sam and Gary rushed up to Regent Terrace, expecting to see their former home gone, destroyed or at very least severely smoke damaged. Unbelievably, their house, and two of the other houses which had experienced paranormal activity had escaped being destroyed. Of the three only one suffered any damage, that being a few burnt timbers and smoke damage. The fire had completely gutted five of the homes in the street; only the three 'haunted' homes remained.

Scawby Crossroads.

The Phantom Coach – Scawby

The village of Scawby, like many places, has changed both geographically and aesthetically over the passage of time. Back in the 1800s, for instance, there was a road just north of the village that led to a crossroads; there was also a lake nearby that no longer exists now either. Though these geographical features may have long since gone, there are reports that those that frequented them in days gone by may still be visiting the area even after their death.

Legend has it that in the nineteenth century a local man drowned in the old lake. His death was blamed on a phantom horseman who is said to drive his coach along the old 'north road'. Locals claimed to hear the galloping hooves of a team of horses and the rattling of the wooden coach wheels as the ghostly horseman sped along the road, laughing maniacally.

It is not clear whether the unfortunate man who drowned was killed by the horseman whilst he was 'of this earth' or if he was killed by the ghost of the horseman. Either way, it is said that an apparition of a man haunts the former site of the lake. Perhaps it is the man who met his untimely death in its icy-cold waters following his encounter with the phantom horseman.

The Haunted Hoard – Lidgett's Gap – Scawby/Sturton

Lidgett's Gap was situated at the four crossroads between Sturton and Scawby. The 'Gap' received its name from the local people who named it after Captain Lidgett, who was an officer serving under Oliver Cromwell during the English Civil War in the 1600s. With the landscape and roads having changed considerably over the past 400 years, the corner formed by the A18 and A15, between Scawby and Sturton, has since inherited the name.

Local legend has it that there is hidden treasure (possibly buried in Captain Lidgett's time) under the earth somewhere around Lidgett's Gap near an old ash tree. Unfortunately for treasure hunters, however, the hoard is said to be guarded by a boggard.

A boggard (or boggart) is the name given to a supernatural spirit or spectre that haunts a particular place. In Northern England it was believed that a boggard should never be named as once it was it could never be reasoned with, placated or controlled. Such a creature would surely not be named in this case then with the locals in North Lincolnshire being a very superstitious lot during this period of history. As such entities were said to reside in dark enclosed places, perhaps it is not inconceivable that this particular spirit was said to hide in the ash tree waiting for potential treasure hunters. Whether the treasure, or indeed the boggard, can still be found at Lidgett's Gap remains to be seen.

Legend says that a horde is buried at Scawby. This image shows Edward Kelly, one of the most famous figures in English occult history; Edward, an alchemist and necromancer, hoped that spirits would reveal to him the location of various hidden treasures. (Courtesy of Liam Quin, www.fromoldbooks.org)

The Man in Black — Winteringham

A very eerie and bizarre sighting of a ghost took place in Winteringham in the 1980s. The incident took place at the bottom of Sutton's Hill, which is also known to the local people as Hewde Lane.

A young woman was walking home on a foggy day when she had the feeling she was being followed, and as she continued her journey home the feeling of unease increased. As she reached the base of Sutton's Hill she turned around and her fears were confirmed: through the fog the woman saw a tall male figure dressed in black. Fearing for her safety, she ran home as fast as she could and locked herself in the house. Still unable to settle, the woman looked out of the window, only to see that the figure had followed her and, as she described it, was observing her from the road outside. After a short while the phantom man in black simply vanished before her eyes.

This alarming spectre is still said to frequent the area on foggy days.

The Leaky Causeway Calf — Wrawby Road — Wrawby

A most unusual apparition was reported on the Wrawby Road between Brigg and Wrawby towards the end of the nineteenth century. Several travellers related the tale of seeing the ghost of a white calf, which they claimed attempted to lure them into the bog at the side of the road.

Following the relating of these accounts the spectral beast became known to the locals as 'the lacky casey calf', which translates into the leaky or wet causeway calf. Although reports of this strange haunting have long since ceased, the phantom calf may one day be seen again along this stretch of road...

Online Paranormal Resources
And Information

Information and contact details can be found at the relevant websites; information correct at time of going to press.

Barton Ghost Walks: http://www.visitnorthlincolnshire.com/visit.php
Baysgarth House Museum: http://www.culture24.org.uk/yh000033
Brigg Ghost Walks: http://briggbash.org.uk/ghosts.php
Epworth Ghost Walks: http://www.visitnorthlincolnshire.com/visit.php
Epworth Old Rectory: http://www.epwortholdrectory.org.uk
Gainsborough Old Hall: http://www.gainsboroughholdhall.co.uk
Gainsthorpe: http://www.english-heritage.org.uk/server/show/nav.16982
Jacky Newcomb: http://jackynewcomb.webeden.co.uk
Jason Day: http://www.jasonday.co.uk
North Lincolnshire Museum: http://www.northlincs.gov.uk/NorthLincs/leisure/
      museums
Old Nick Theatre: http://www.gainsboroughtheatrecompany.com/index.htm
Peter Underwood: http://www.peterunderwood.org.uk
Phantom Encounters Limited: http://www.phantomencounters.co.uk
The Society For Psychical Research: http://www.spr.ac.uk
Thornton Abbey:http://www.english-heritage.org.uk/server.php?show=nav.11808
White Noise Paranormal Radio: http://www.whitenoiseparanormalradio.co.uk and
      http://www.blogtalkradio.com/famously-haunted

Other titles published by The History Press

Haunted Sheffield

MR P. DREADFUL

The tales contained in this book are told by the Steel City Tours ghost walkers themselves, collected over the years and now brought together here for all to read. There are tales of haunted pubs like the Brown Bear pub in Norfolk Street, where a ghostly coachman is a regular visitor, the Graduate in Surrey Street where a lady in black walks through the kitchen and exits through the wall, and the Museum pub in Orchard Square, where a ghost knocks over the beer glasses! Ghostly encounters are described in the most unlikely places, including the Central Library, the Cathedral, Boots the Chemists and the Roxy nightclub.

978 0 7524 4195 5

Haunted Lincoln

DAVID BRANDON

The half-timbered buildings that cling to the steep streets and narrow lanes of the cit of Lincoln groan under the weight of thousands of years of history. Not surprisingly, this ancient city is rife with tales of spectral spirits and ghastly ghouls. Even the more workaday areas can boast haunted pubs, residences and mysterious goings-on in the theatre. In this book the city and surrounding area is explored, with reports of dancir stones, roadside apparitions and omens of death in deserted churchyards.

978 07 524 4891 6

Haunted York

RUPERT MATTHEWS

This is a terrifying collection of true-life tales of ghosts, poltergeists and spirits of all kinds in the streets, buildings and graveyards of York. Drawing on historical and contemporary sources, *Haunted York* contains a chilling range of ghostly phenomena. From the medieval stonemason who haunts York Minster to a re-incarnation myster at St Mary's Church, the spectres of King's Manor, Micklegate Bar and Exhibition Square and the many spirits to be found in the city's public houses, this phenomenal gathering of ghostly goings-on is bound to captivate anyone interested in the supernatural history of York.

978 0 7524 4910 4

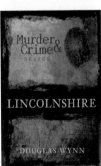

Murder & Crime in Lincolnshire

DOUGLAS WYNN

These tales from Lincolnshire's forgotten past are testament to the sinister side of the county's coastal resorts and inland market towns. Retold for a new generation are shocking stories of drunken brawls in towns, death from poison and jealous rages. Mixing genuine historical documents with contemporary photography to show the scenes where these disturbing dramas were played out, Wynn's collection of true crin provides a mesmerising evocation of the past. It is sure to haunt the imagination of any reader with an interest in the darker history of Lincolnshire.

978 0 7524 4864 0

Visit our website and discover thousands of other History Press books.

www.thehistorypress.co.uk

The
History
Press